MathFlare

Name: ________________________

Class: __________

Teacher: ________________________

Introduction

As parents and educators, we recognize the pivotal role mathematics plays in shaping a child's academic journey and future success. Yet, the path to mathematical proficiency can often seem daunting, fraught with challenges and complexities. That's where the transformative power of MathFlare Workbooks shine through, illuminating the way forward with clarity, precision, and purpose.

Introducing MathFlare Workbooks – a beacon of guidance, a testament to excellence, and a catalyst for achievement. Crafted with meticulous care and expertise, MathFlare Workbooks stand as paragons of educational excellence, designed to nurture young minds, ignite a passion for learning, and develop a deep-rooted understanding of mathematical concepts.

Picture this: your child eagerly delves into the pages of Mathflare Workbook, greeted by a step-by-step guide illuminated with vivid examples that demystify complex mathematical concepts. With each turn of the page, they embark on a journey of discovery, encountering thoughtfully curated practice questions that reinforce learning and hone problem-solving skills. And when they unveil the answers to those very questions, a sense of accomplishment blossoms within them – a tangible reward for their hard work and dedication.

But MathFlare Workbooks are more than just tools for learning; they are pathways to comprehension, fostering a deep-seated understanding of mathematical concepts through a sequential, logical flow. From fundamental principles to advanced problem-solving strategies, every chapter builds upon the last, ensuring a robust foundation upon which future knowledge can be constructed.

As parents, we yearn for nothing more than to see our children thrive, to witness the spark of inspiration ignited within them as they conquer academic challenges with confidence and poise. MathFlare Workbooks serve as partners in this noble endeavor, offering not just practice questions, but the keys to unlocking a world of opportunity.

And for teachers, MathFlare Workbooks stand as invaluable allies in the quest to cultivate mathematical proficiency in the classroom. With answers readily available, instructors can focus on guiding and nurturing their students, confident in the knowledge that MathFlare Workbooks provide a solid framework upon which to build.

In the pages of MathFlare Workbooks, we find not just the promise of academic excellence, but the seeds of a brighter tomorrow. So let us embrace the power of mathematics, let us champion the journey of learning, and let us pave the way for a generation of young minds poised to shape the world. With MathFlare Workbooks as our guide, the possibilities are infinite, and the future, bright.

Table of Contents

Geometry and Statistics	
Mean and Median, Mode and Range	1
Area and Perimeter	16
Volume and Surface Area	36
Pythagorean Theorem	51

MathFlare
MATH WORKBOOK
Grade 2
Addition Subtraction
Multiplication
Place Value and Expanded Notations
Geometry
Step by Step Guide and Essential Practice with Answers
MathFlare Publishing

MathFlare
MATH WORKBOOK
Grade 2-3
Addition Subtraction
Multiplication and Division
Place Value and Expanded Notations
Geometry
Step by Step Guide and Essential Practice with Answers
MathFlare Publishing

MathFlare
MATH WORKBOOK
Grade 3
Multiplication and Division
Decimals
Place Value and Expanded Notations
Fractions and Geometry
Step by Step Guide and Essential Practice with Answers

MathFlare
MATH WORKBOOK
Grade 1
Counting and Numbers
Addition and Subtraction
Place Value and Expanded Notations
Understanding Time
Step by Step Guide and Essential Practice with Answers
MathFlare Publishing

MathFlare
MATH WORKBOOK
Grade 1-2
Counting and Numbers
Addition and Subtraction
Place Value and Expanded Notations
Understanding Time
Step by Step Guide and Essential Practice with Answers
MathFlare Publishing

MathFlare
MATH WORKBOOK
Grade 3-4
Addition Subtraction
Multiplication Division
Place Value and Expanded Notations
Fractions and Geometry
Step by Step Guide and Essential Practice with Answers
MathFlare Publishing

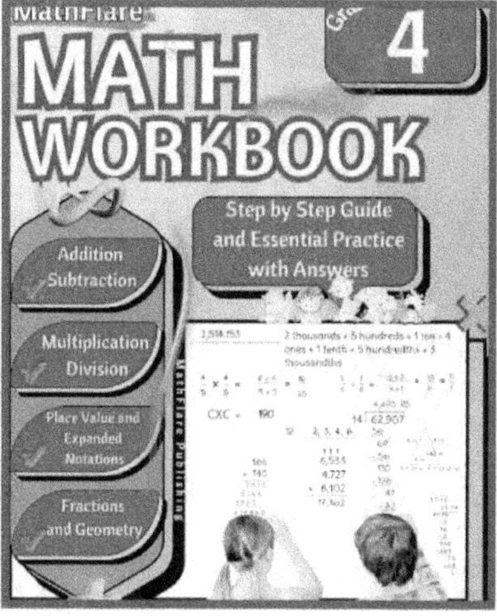

MathFlare
MATH WORKBOOK
Grade 4
Addition Subtraction
Multiplication Division
Place Value and Expanded Notations
Fractions and Geometry
Step by Step Guide and Essential Practice with Answers
MathFlare Publishing

MathFlare
MATH WORKBOOK
Grade 4-5
Multiplication Division
Place Value and Expanded Notations
Fractions and Geometry
Unit Conversion
Step by Step Guide and Essential Practice with Answers
MathFlare Publishing

MathFlare
MATH WORKBOOK
5
Step by Step Guide and Essential Practice with Answers
Multiplication Division
Place Value and Expanded Notations
Fractions and Geometry
Unit Conversion
MathFlare Publishing

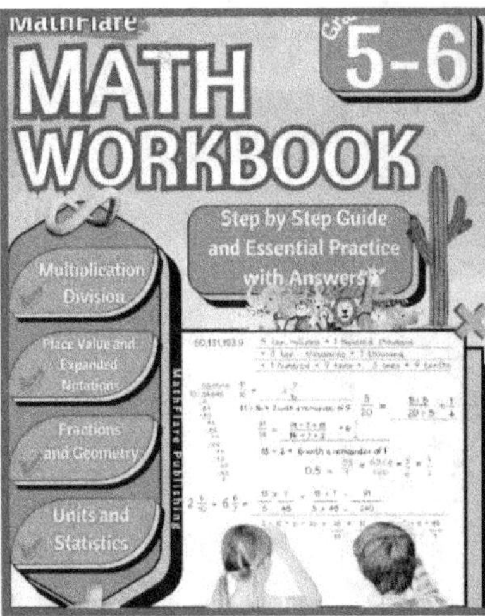
MathFlare
MATH WORKBOOK
5-6
Step by Step Guide and Essential Practice with Answers
Multiplication Division
Place Value and Expanded Notations
Fractions and Geometry
Units and Statistics
MathFlare Publishing

MathFlare
MATH WORKBOOK
6
Step by Step Guide and Essential Practice with Answers
Integers and Statistics
Arithmetic and Pre-Algebra
Fractions and Geometry
Ratio and Percentage
MathFlare Publishing

MathFlare
MATH WORKBOOK
6-7
Step by Step Guide and Essential Practice with Answers
Arithmetic and Pre-Algebra
Ratio, Percent Proportion
Geometry
Statistics
MathFlare Publishing

MathFlare
MATH WORKBOOK
7
Step by Step Guide and Essential Practice with Answers
Pre-Algebra
Ratio, Percent Proportion
Geometry
Statistics
MathFlare Publishing

MathFlare
MATH WORKBOOK
7-8
Step by Step Guide and Essential Practice with Answers
Pre-Algebra
Ratio, Percent Proportion
Geometry and Cartesian Plane
Statistics
MathFlare Publishing

MathFlare
MATH WORKBOOK
8-9
Step by Step Guide and Essential Practice with Answers
Pre-Algebra
Ratio, Proportion and Percentage
Linear Equations
Geometry and Cartesian Plane
MathFlare Publishing

MathFlare
MATH WORKBOOK
8
Step by Step Guide and Essential Practice with Answers
Pre-Algebra
Percentage
Linear Equations
Geometry
MathFlare Publishing

Statistics

Mean

The mean, also known as the average, is a measure of central tendency.

To find the mean of a set of numbers:

- Add up all the numbers in the set.
- Divide the sum by the total count of numbers in the set.

For example: consider the set of numbers: 70, 72, 49, 69, 27, 76.

$$\text{Mean} = \frac{70 + 72 + 49 + 69 + 27 + 76}{6}$$

$$= \frac{363}{6} = 60.5$$

Median

The median is a measure of central tendency that represents the middle value of a dataset when the values are arranged in ascending or descending order.

To find the median of a set of numbers:

- Arrange the numbers in ascending or descending order.
- If the total count of numbers is odd, the median is the middle value.
- If the total count of numbers is even, the median is the average of the two middle values.

For example: consider the set of numbers: 70, 72, 49, 69, 27, 76.

$$27, 49, 69, 70, 72, 76$$

$$\text{Median} = \frac{69 + 70}{2} = \frac{139}{2} = 69.5$$

Mode

The mode in statistics refers to the value that appears most frequently in a given set of data.

Let's consider the following set of numbers:

$$\{2, 4, 4, 5, 6, 6, 6, 7, 8, 8\}$$

In this set, the number 6 appears three times, more than any other number. Therefore, the mode of this dataset is 6.

It's possible for a dataset to have more than one mode if two or more numbers appear with the same highest frequency. In such cases, the dataset is considered multimodal. If no number repeats, the dataset is considered to have no mode.

For example:

$$\{2, 4, 4, 4, 5, 6, 6, 6, 7, 8, 8\}$$

In this date set, 4 and 6 appear three times. Therefore, this dataset is multimodal.

Range

In statistics, the range refers to the difference between the largest and smallest values in a dataset. It represents the spread or variability of the data.

For example, consider the dataset $\{ 68, 13, 30, 18, 45, 76, 11\}$:

To calculate the range:

1. Arrange the data points in ascending order.

$$11, 13, 18, 30, 45, 68, 76$$

2. Subtract the smallest value from the largest value.

- The smallest value is 11.
- The largest value is 76.

$$\text{Range} = \text{Largest value} - \text{smallest value} = 76 - 11 = 65.$$

Geometry

Area and Perimeter

The area of a shape represents the amount of space it occupies. The perimeter of a shape is the total distance around its outer edge.

Area of Rectangle

For a square, since all four sides are equal, we only need to know the length of one side to find its area. We can calculate the area of a square by multiplying the length of one side by itself (squared). So, if the length of one side of the square is 's', then the area (A) is given by:

$$A = s \times s$$

4 in

4 in

$$A = 4 \times 4$$

$$A = 16$$

Perimeter of Rectangle

For a square, since all four sides are equal, we can find the perimeter by adding up the lengths of all four sides. If 's' represents the length of one side, then the perimeter (P) is given by:

$$P = 4 \times s$$

$$P = 4 \times 4$$

$$P = 16$$

Area of Triangle:

The area of a triangle represents the amount of space enclosed within its three sides. The formula for calculating the area of a triangle depends on the type of triangle. For a general triangle, we use the formula:

$$A = \frac{1}{2} \times base \times height$$

Where:

- A represents the area of the triangle.

- The base is the length of any one side of the triangle.

- The height is the perpendicular distance from the base to the opposite vertex.

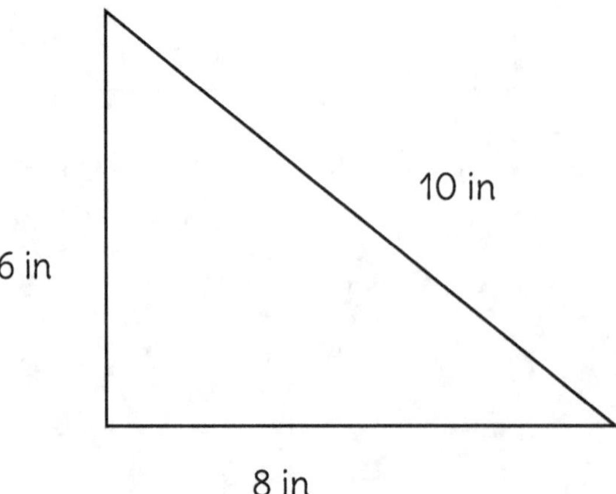

$$A = \frac{1}{2} \times \text{base} \times \text{height}$$

$$A = \frac{1}{2} \times 6 \times 8$$

$$A = \frac{1}{2} \times 48$$

$$A = 24$$

Perimeter of Triangle:

The perimeter of a triangle is the total length of its three sides. To find the perimeter, we simply add the lengths of all three sides together:

$$P = \text{side1} + \text{side2} + \text{side3}$$

$$P = 6 + 8 + 10$$

$$P = 24$$

Equilateral Triangle

An equilateral triangle is a triangle in which all three sides are equal in length. To find the area and perimeter of an equilateral triangle, we can use the following formulas:

- Area (A): $\frac{\sqrt{3}}{4} \times a^2$ where a is the length of one side of the equilateral triangle.

- Perimeter (P): $P = 3a$ where a is the length of one side of the equilateral triangle.

Let's solve a problem:

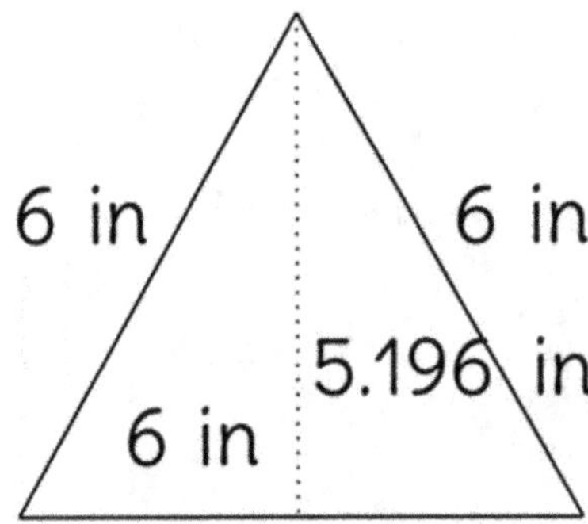

Area of Equilateral Triangle:

$$\text{Area (A): } \frac{\sqrt{3}}{4} \times (6)^2$$

$$\text{Area (A): } \frac{\sqrt{3}}{4} \times 36$$

$$\text{Area (A): } \frac{36\sqrt{3}}{4}$$

$$\text{Area (A): } \frac{36(1.73)}{4}$$

$$\text{Area (A): } \frac{62.35}{4}$$

$$\text{Area (A): } 15.59 \text{ in}^2$$

Perimeter of Equilateral Triangle:

$$P = 3a$$

$$P = 3(6) = 18$$

MathFlare - Geometry and Statistics

Isosceles Triangle

An isosceles triangle is a triangle with at least two sides of equal length. The angles opposite the equal sides are also equal.

Area of Isosceles Triangle

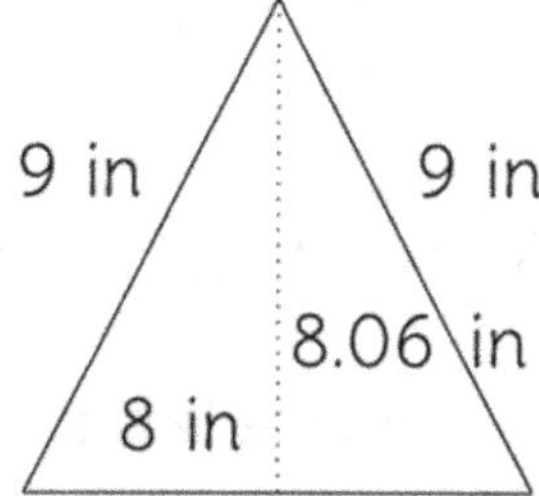

$$A = \frac{1}{2} \times base \times height$$

$$A = \frac{1}{2} \times 8 \times 8$$

$$A = \frac{1}{2} \times 64$$

$$A = 32$$

Perimeter of Isosceles Triangle

The perimeter of a triangle is the total length of its three sides. To find the perimeter, we simply add the lengths of all three sides together:

$$P = side1 + side2 + side3$$

$$P = 9 + 9 + 8$$

$$P = 26$$

Scalene Triangle

A scalene triangle is a triangle with no equal sides and no equal angles. The formula for finding various properties of a scalene triangle is as follows:

Area (A): The area of a scalene triangle can be calculated using Heron's formula, which is given by:

$$A = \sqrt{s(s-a)(s-b)(s-c)}$$

where s is the semi-perimeter of the triangle,

and a, b, and c are the lengths of its three sides.

Perimeter (P): The perimeter of a scalene triangle is the sum of the lengths of its three sides.

$$P = side1 + side2 + side3$$

Let's find the Area and Perimeter of a Scalene Triangle:

15.6 cm   16.6 cm

15.52 cm

7.7 cm

Area (A): First, we calculate the semi-perimeter (s):

$$S = \frac{a+b+c}{2} = \frac{15.6 + 16.6 + 7.7}{2} = \frac{39.8}{2} = 19.9 \text{ cm}$$

Heron's formula to find the area:

$$A = \sqrt{s(s-a)(s-b)(s-c)}$$

$$A = \sqrt{19.9\,(19.9-15.6)(19.9-16.6)(19.9-7.7)}$$

$$A = \sqrt{19.9 \times 4.3 \times 3.3 \times 12.2}$$

$$A = \sqrt{3445} \approx 59$$

Perimeter (P):

$$P = side1 + side2 + side3$$

$$P = 15.6 + 16.6 + 7.7$$

$$P = 39.8$$

Area and Perimeter of an L-shape

The L-shaped figure typically consists of two rectangles joined together to form an L-shape. To find the area and perimeter of an L-shaped figure, we will need to calculate the areas and perimeters of each rectangle and then combine them.

Area=Area of Rectangle 1 + Area of Rectangle 2

Perimeter=Perimeter of Rectangle 1 + Perimeter of Rectangle 2

Let's find the Area and Perimeter of an L-shape:

Area of L-Shape

$$\text{Area 1} = 4.38 \times 4.5 = 19.7 \text{ cm}^2$$

$$\text{Area 2} = 11.28 \times 6.54 = 73.7 \text{ cm}^2$$

$$\text{Area} = 19.7 + 73.7$$

$$\text{Area} = 93.481 \text{ cm}^2$$

Perimeter of L-Shape

$$P = 11.28 + 6.54 + 6.78 + 4.38 + 4.5 + 10.92$$

$$P = 44.4 \text{ cm}$$

Area and Perimeter of U-shape

U-shape is basically composed of three rectangles, we'll need to calculate the area and perimeter of each rectangle separately and then sum them up.

Area of the U-shape:

The total area (A) of the U-shape is the sum of the areas of the three rectangles:

$$A = A1 + A2 + A3$$

Perimeter of the U-shape: The total perimeter (P) of the U-shape is the sum of the perimeters of the three rectangles:

$$P = P1 + P2 + P3$$

Let's find the area and perimeter of the following U-shape:

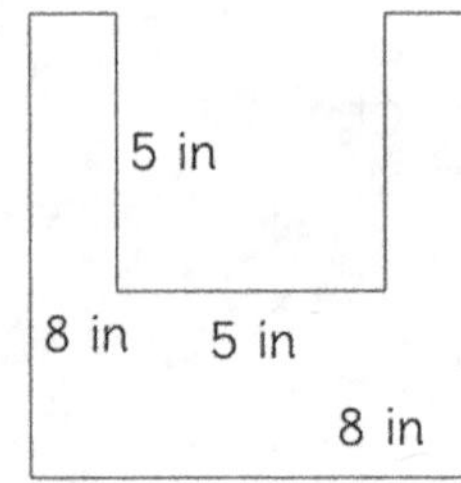

Area:

$$A1 = 8 \times 1.5 = 12 + A2 = 3 \times 5 = 15 + A3 = 8 \times 1.5 = 12$$

$$= 12 + 15 + 12$$

$$= 39 \ in^2$$

Perimeter:

$$2 \times 8 + 2 \times 5 + 2 \times 8$$

$$= 16 + 10 + 16$$

$$= 42$$

Area and Perimeter of T-shape

The T-shape consists of two rectangles joined together to form a T-like structure.

Area of the T-shape:

To find the total area of the T-shape, we need to calculate the areas of both rectangles and then add them together.

$$\text{Area of Rectangle 1} = \text{Length} \times \text{Width}$$

$$\text{Area of Rectangle 2} = \text{Length} \times \text{Width}$$

$$\text{Total Area} = \text{Area of Rectangle 1} + \text{Area of Rectangle 2}$$

The perimeter of the T-shape is the sum of the perimeters of the two rectangles, minus the length of the overlapping side:

$$\text{Perimeter} = 2(l1+w1) + 2(l2+w2) - (w1-w2)$$

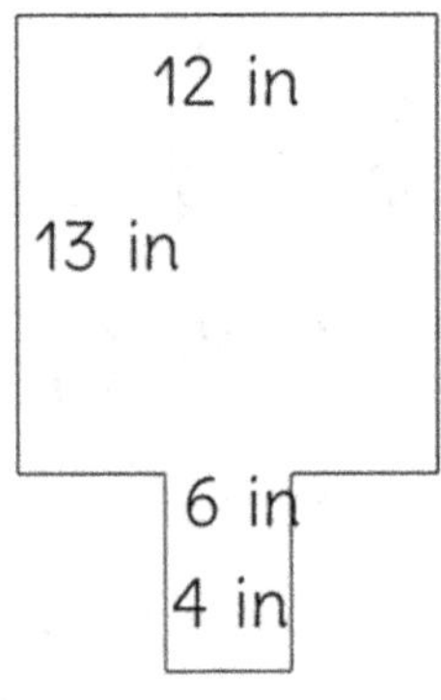

Area= 12 × 13 + 6 × 4

Area= 156 + 24

Area= 180 in²

Perimeter= 2(12+13) +2(6+4) – (12-4)

Perimeter=2(25) + 2(10) – 8

Perimeter= 50 + 20 – 8

Perimeter= 62 in²

Area and Perimeter of Parallelogram

A parallelogram is a four-sided polygon with opposite sides that are parallel and equal in length. To find the area and perimeter of a parallelogram, we use specific formulas based on its dimensions.

For example:

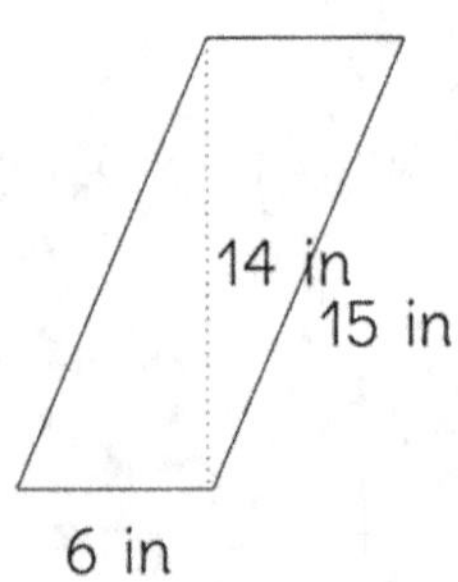

Let's denote:

- The length of one side of the parallelogram as $a = 15$.

- The length of an adjacent side (parallel to a) $b = 6$.

- The height of the parallelogram (perpendicular distance between the two parallel sides) as $h=14$

Area of Parallelogram

$$\text{Area} = \text{Base} \times \text{Height}$$

$$\text{Area} = 6 \times 14$$

$$\text{Area} = 84$$

Perimeter of Parallelogram

$$2(a + b)$$

$$= 2(15+6)$$

$$= 2(21)$$

$$= 42$$

Area and Perimeter of Trapezoids

A trapezoid is a quadrilateral with at least one pair of parallel sides. To find the area and perimeter of a trapezoid, we use specific formulas based on its dimensions.

For example:

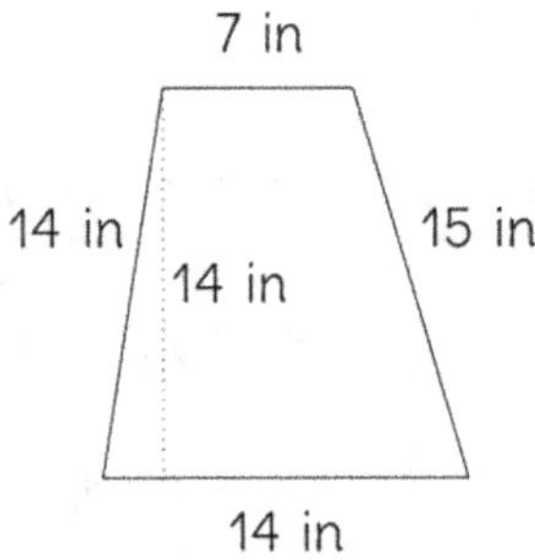

Let's denote:

- The lengths of the parallel sides of the trapezoid as $a = 7$ and $b = 14$.

- The lengths of the non-parallel sides as $c = 14$ and $d = 15$.

- The height of the trapezoid (the perpendicular distance between the parallel sides) as $h=14$.

Area of the Trapezoid:

The area of a trapezoid is given by the formula:

$$\text{Area} = \frac{1}{2} \times \text{Height} \times (\text{Sum of the lengths of the parallel sides})$$

$$\text{Area} = \frac{1}{2} \times h \times (a + b)$$

$$\text{Area} = \frac{1}{2} \times 14 \times (7 + 14)$$

$$\text{Area} = \frac{1}{2} \times 14 \times 21$$

$$\text{Area} = 147 \text{ in}^2$$

Perimeter of the Trapezoid:

$$\text{Perimeter} = 7 + 14 + 14 + 15$$

$$= 50 \text{ in}^2$$

MathFlare - Geometry and Statistics

<u>Pythagorean Theorem</u>

The Pythagorean Theorem is a fundamental principle in geometry that relates the lengths of the sides of a right triangle. It states that in any right triangle, the square of the length of the hypotenuse (the side opposite the right angle) is equal to the sum of the squares of the lengths of the other two sides.

$$a2 + b2 = c2$$

Let's use the Pythagorean Theorem to find the length of the hypotenuse (c) when $a=44$ and $b=78$.

$$c^2 = 44^2 + 78^2$$
$$c^2 = 1936 + 6084 \qquad c = \sqrt{8020}$$
$$c^2 = 8020 \qquad\qquad c \approx 89.554$$

<u>Volume and surface Area</u>

Volume refers to the amount of space occupied by a three-dimensional object. For shapes like cubes or rectangular prisms, we calculate volume by multiplying their length, width, and height.

To find the volume V of a rectangular prism, we use the formula:

$$Volume = length \; x \; width \; x \; height$$

Surface Area represents the total area covering all the faces of a three-dimensional object. For shapes like cubes or rectangular prisms, we find the surface area by summing the areas of all its faces.

The formula for surface area SA of a cube or rectangular prism is:

MathFlare - Geometry and Statistics

$$Surface\ Area\ =\ 2lw\ +\ 2lh\ +\ 2wh$$

Where: l is the length, w is the width, and h is the height of the object.

For example: Let's find the Volume and Surface Area of following rectangular prisms:

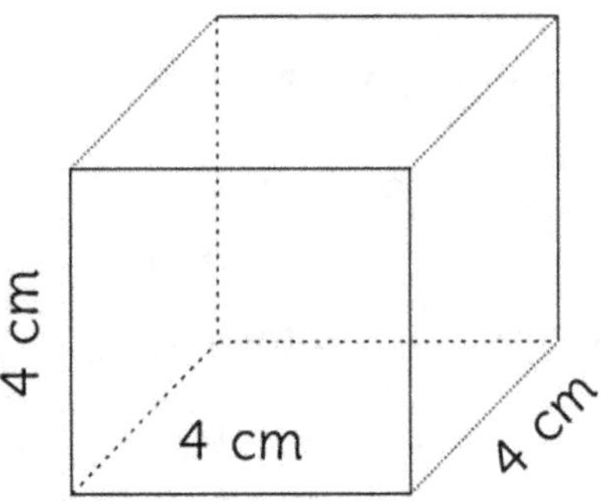

$$Volume\ =\ length\ \times\ width\ \times\ height$$

$$= 4 \times 4 \times 4$$

$$= 64\ cm^2$$

$$Surface\ Area\ =\ 2lw\ +\ 2lh\ +\ 2wh$$

$$= 2(4 \times 4) + 2(4 \times 4) + 2(4 \times 4)$$

$$= 32 + 32 + 32$$

$$= 96\ cm2$$

Different 3D objects have unique formulas for finding their volume and surface area. Here are some common ones:

1. **Cube:**

   - Volume: $V = s^3$ (where s is the length of one side of the cube)

   - Surface area: $SA = 6s^2$

2. Sphere:

- Volume: $V = (\frac{4}{3})\pi r^3$ (where r is the radius of the sphere)

- Surface area: $SA = 4\pi r^2$

3. Cone:

- Volume: $V = (\frac{1}{3})\pi r^2 h$ (where r is the radius of the base and h is the height of the cone)

- Surface area: $SA = \pi r^2 + \pi r \sqrt{(r^2 + h^2)}$

4. Cylinder:

- Volume: $V = \pi r^2 h$ (where r is the radius of the base and h is the height of the cylinder)

- Surface area: $SA = 2\pi r^2 + 2\pi rh$

5. Pyramid:

- Volume: $V = (\frac{1}{3})Bh$ (where B is the area of the base and h is the height of the pyramid)

- Surface area: $SA = B + \frac{1}{2}Pl$ (where P is the perimeter of the base and l is the slant height of the pyramid)

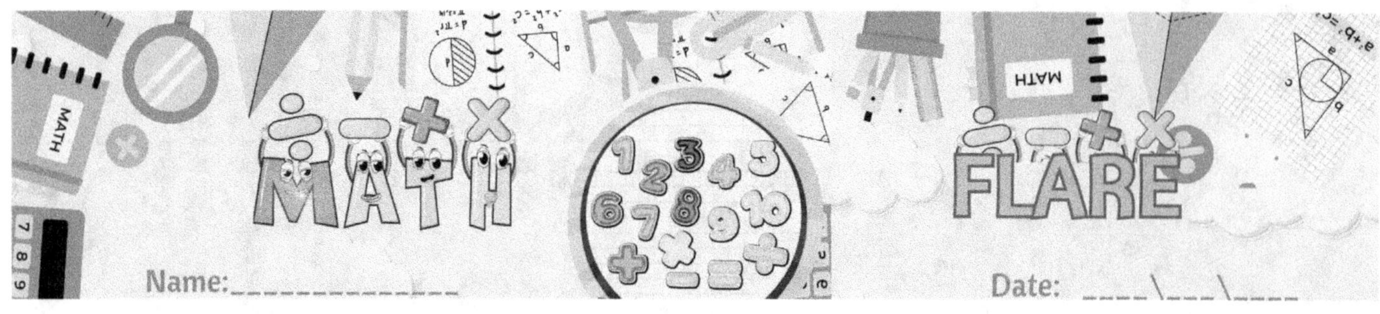

Mean, Median, Mode, and Range

Find the Mean, Median, Mode and Range of the following sets of data.

1. 70, 10, 67, 88, 46, 19

   Mean = _____ Median = _____

   Mode = _____ Range = _____

2. 76, 97, 20, 91, 6, 16

   Mean = _____ Median = _____

   Mode = _____ Range = _____

3. 27, 96, 47, 32, 50, 88

   Mean = _____ Median = _____

   Mode = _____ Range = _____

4. 32, 25, 54, 98, 75, 15, 42

   Mean = _____ Median = _____

   Mode = _____ Range = _____

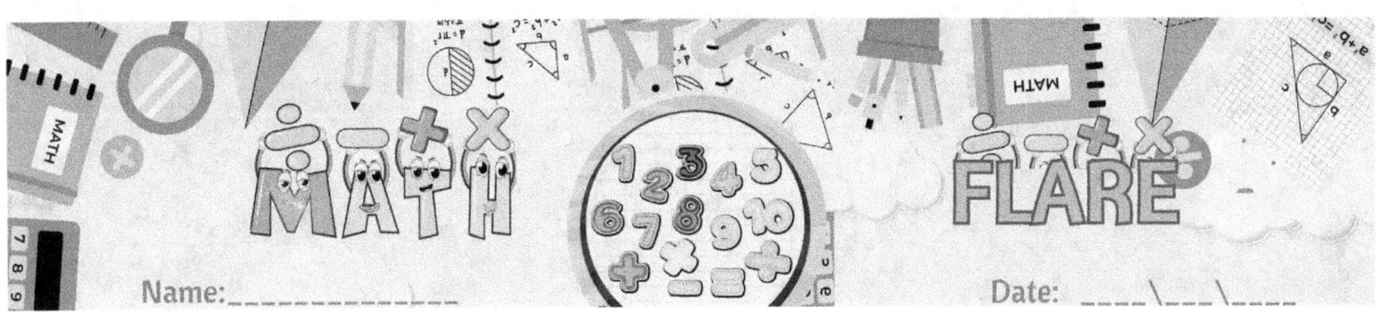

5. 83, 63, 27, 36, 20, 89

   Mean = _____   Median = _____

   Mode = _____   Range = _____

6. 23, 12, 40, 37, 27, 33, 46

   Mean = _____   Median = _____

   Mode = _____   Range = _____

7. 29, 84, 71, 81, 16, 69

   Mean = _____   Median = _____

   Mode = _____   Range = _____

8. 17, 37, 56, 60, 3, 19, 99

   Mean = _____   Median = _____

   Mode = _____   Range = _____

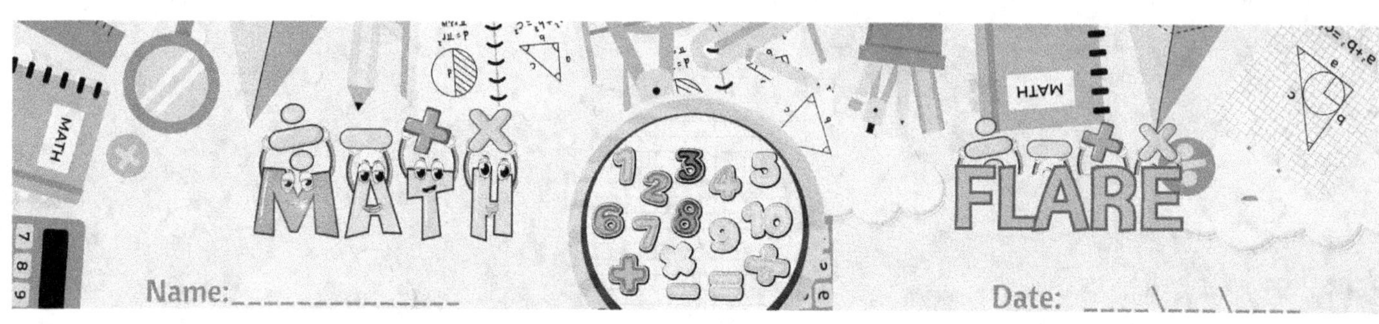

9. 93, 79, 42, 75, 72, 34, 53

Mean = _____ Median = _____

Mode = _____ Range = _____

10. 46, 63, 55, 49, 61, 1, 3

Mean = _____ Median = _____

Mode = _____ Range = _____

11. 82, 5, 86, 59, 20, 98

Mean = _____ Median = _____

Mode = _____ Range = _____

12. 5, 59, 47, 53, 73, 83, 7

Mean = _____ Median = _____

Mode = _____ Range = _____

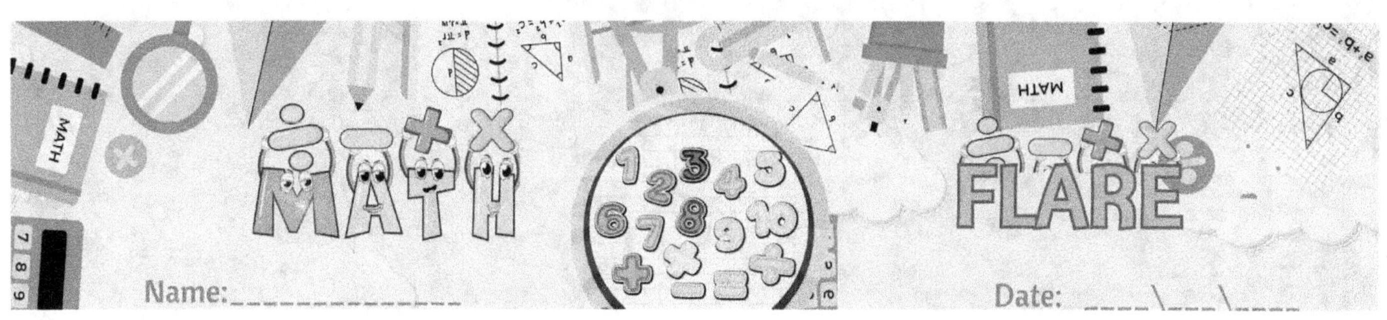

13. 97, 6, 27, 4, 25, 18, 20

Mean = _______   Median = _____

Mode = _______   Range = _____

14. 95, 44, 69, 65, 64, 93

Mean = _______   Median = _____

Mode = _______   Range = _____

15. 80, 99, 65, 30, 23, 21

Mean = _____   Median = _____

Mode = _____   Range = _____

16. 15, 66, 35, 33, 70, 2

Mean = _______   Median = _____

Mode = _______   Range = _____

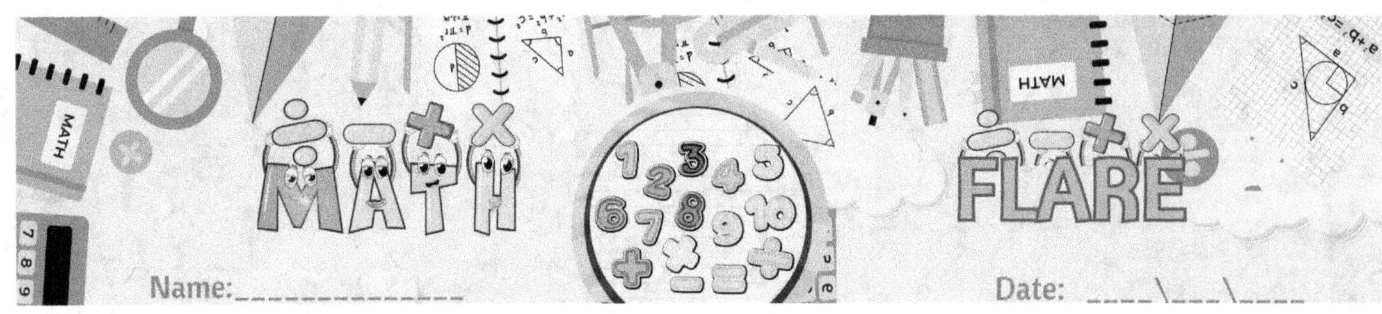

17. 83, 20, 95, 35, 32, 88, 3

Mean = _______   Median = _____

Mode = _______   Range = _____

18. 88, 28, 55, 41, 37, 52

Mean = _______   Median = _____

Mode = _______   Range = _____

19. 25, 44, 80, 7, 38, 35, 22

Mean = _______   Median = _____

Mode = _______   Range = _____

20. 94, 27, 19, 5, 93, 18, 31

Mean = _______   Median = _____

Mode = _______   Range = _____

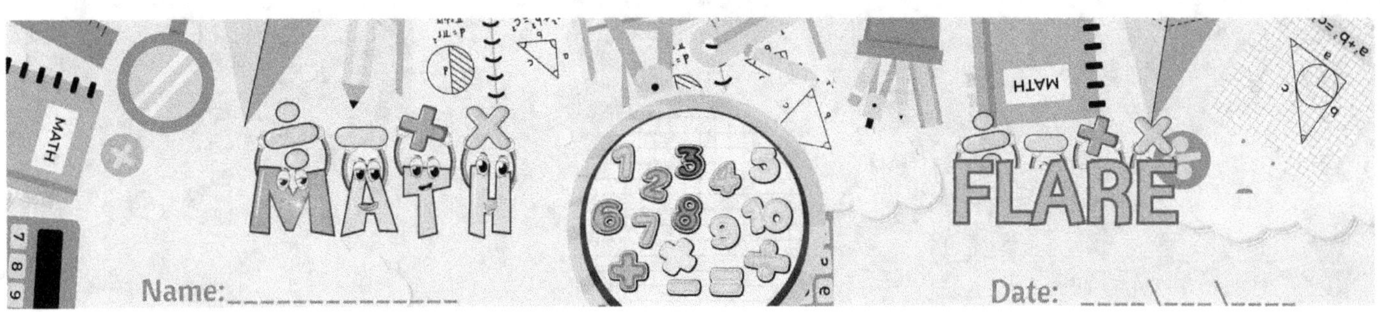

21. 53, 68, 40, 62, 73, 57, 2

Mean = _______   Median = _____

Mode = _______   Range = _____

22. 41, 97, 24, 61, 13, 80

Mean = _______   Median = _____

Mode = _______   Range = _____

23. 62, 75, 65, 25, 59, 29

Mean = _____   Median = _____

Mode = _____   Range = _____

24. 78, 97, 76, 35, 59, 97, 97

Mean = _____   Median = _____

Mode = _____   Range = _____

25. 49, 7, 57, 2, 91, 41

Mean = _______   Median = _____

Mode = _______   Range = _____

26. 14, 58, 50, 21, 87, 93, 67

Mean = _______   Median = _____

Mode = _______   Range = _____

27. 80, 50, 83, 46, 57, 46

Mean = _______   Median = _____

Mode = _______   Range = _____

28. 25, 55, 59, 19, 61, 94, 45

Mean = _______   Median = _____

Mode = _______   Range = _____

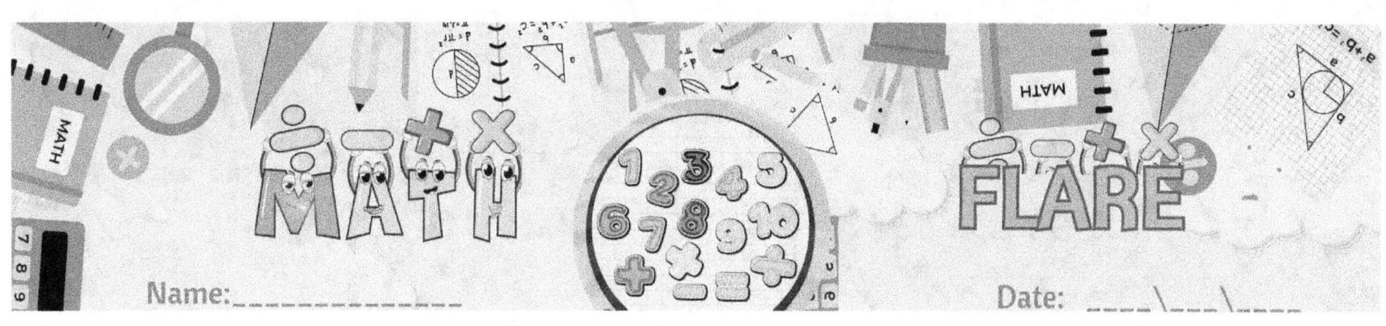

29. 65, 40, 34, 76, 34, 80

Mean = _______   Median = _____
Mode = _______   Range = _____

30. 65, 75, 8, 95, 84, 96, 32

Mean = _____   Median = _____
Mode = _____   Range = _____

31. 21, 99, 23, 13, 55, 78

Mean = _______   Median = _____
Mode = _______   Range = _____

32. 32, 91, 49, 29, 15, 31

Mean = _______   Median = _____
Mode = _______   Range = _____

33. 78, 13, 72, 43, 89, 87

    Mean = _______   Median = _____
    Mode = _______   Range = _____

34. 96, 8, 47, 75, 74, 25

    Mean = _______   Median = _____
    Mode = _______   Range = _____

35. 74, 87, 7, 28, 92, 72

    Mean = _____   Median = _____
    Mode = _____   Range = _____

36. 54, 99, 50, 25, 26, 26

    Mean = _______   Median = _____
    Mode = _______   Range = _____

37. 33, 47, 64, 83, 62, 53, 17

    Mean = _______   Median = _____

    Mode = _______   Range = _____

38. 12, 19, 46, 56, 68, 93, 33

    Mean = _______   Median = _____

    Mode = _______   Range = _____

39. 19, 9, 88, 89, 85, 45, 26

    Mean = _______   Median = _____

    Mode = _______   Range = _____

40. 98, 38, 68, 71, 4, 99

    Mean = _______   Median = _____

    Mode = _______   Range = _____

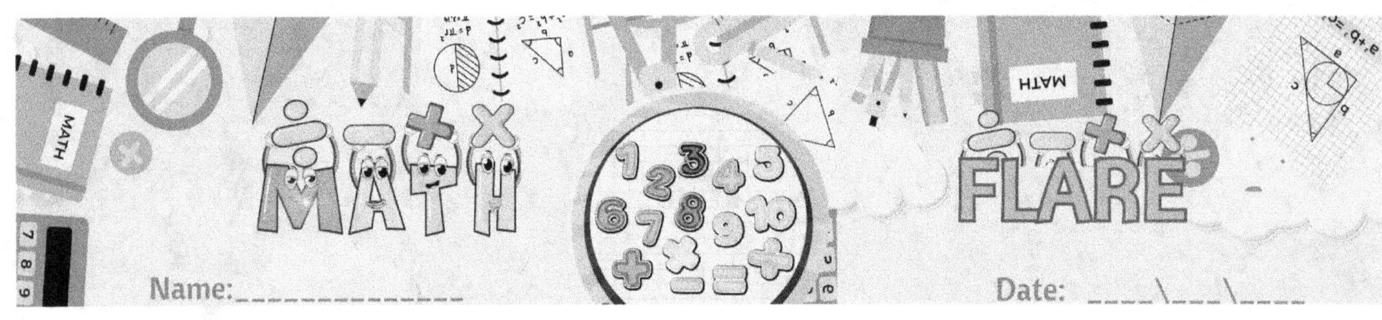

41. 76, 74, 16, 80, 53, 87

Mean = _______   Median = _____

Mode = _______   Range = _____

42. 46, 11, 43, 23, 14, 45, 93

Mean = _______   Median = _____

Mode = _______   Range = _____

43. 59, 62, 6, 29, 32, 39, 34

Mean = _______   Median = _____

Mode = _______   Range = _____

44. 60, 53, 46, 12, 60, 39

Mean = _____   Median = _____

Mode = _____   Range = _____

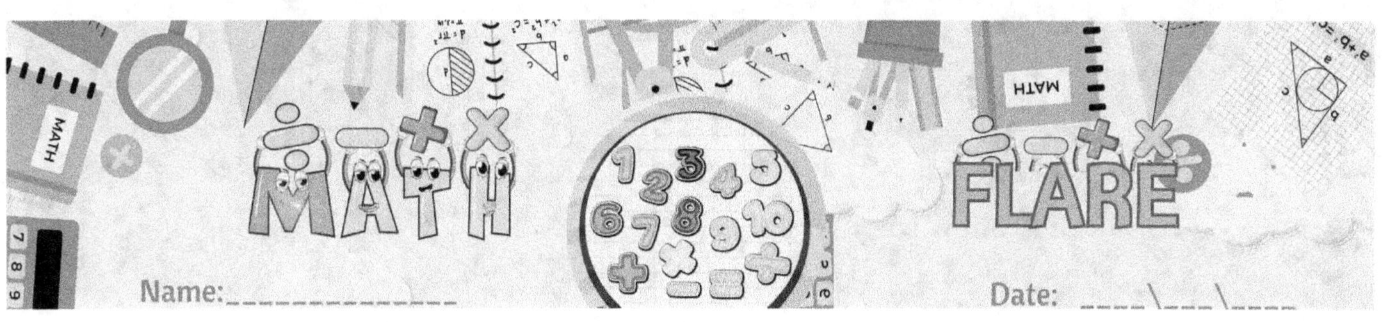

45. 81, 1, 34, 9, 96, 12

Mean = _______   Median = _____
Mode = _______   Range = _____

46. 58, 54, 40, 37, 4, 65, 3

Mean = _______   Median = _____
Mode = _______   Range = _____

47. 80, 48, 23, 76, 85, 75

Mean = _____   Median = _____
Mode = _____   Range = _____

48. 44, 92, 85, 63, 92, 10

Mean = _______   Median = _____
Mode = _______   Range = _____

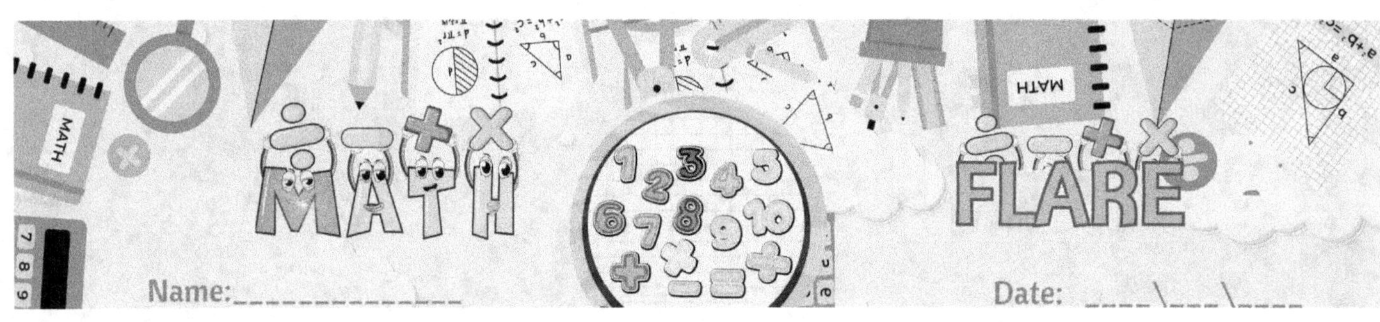

49. 36, 32, 69, 40, 24, 29

Mean = _______   Median = _____

Mode = _______   Range = _____

50. 5, 20, 15, 6, 45, 76

Mean = _______   Median = _____

Mode = _______   Range = _____

51. 34, 27, 2, 86, 40, 20, 25

Mean = _______   Median = _____

Mode = _______   Range = _____

52. 2, 63, 29, 59, 86, 37, 77

Mean = _______   Median = _____

Mode = _______   Range = _____

Name:_________________   Date: ____________

53. 60, 36, 17, 47, 95, 38

Mean = _______   Median = _____
Mode = _______   Range = _____

54. 42, 98, 60, 80, 89, 14, 17

Mean = _______   Median = _____
Mode = _______   Range = _____

55. 9, 99, 45, 88, 74, 3, 47

Mean = _______   Median = _____
Mode = _______   Range = _____

56. 42, 58, 74, 58, 52, 66, 38

Mean = _______   Median = _____
Mode = _______   Range = _____

57. 91, 46, 8, 73, 82, 3, 46

    Mean = _______   Median = _____

    Mode = _______   Range = _____

58. 68, 68, 4, 67, 11, 8

    Mean = _______   Median = _____

    Mode = _______   Range = _____

59. 35, 35, 67, 21, 97, 26

    Mean = _______   Median = _____

    Mode = _______   Range = _____

60. 3, 17, 3, 19, 41, 84

    Mean = _______   Median = _____

    Mode = _______   Range = _____

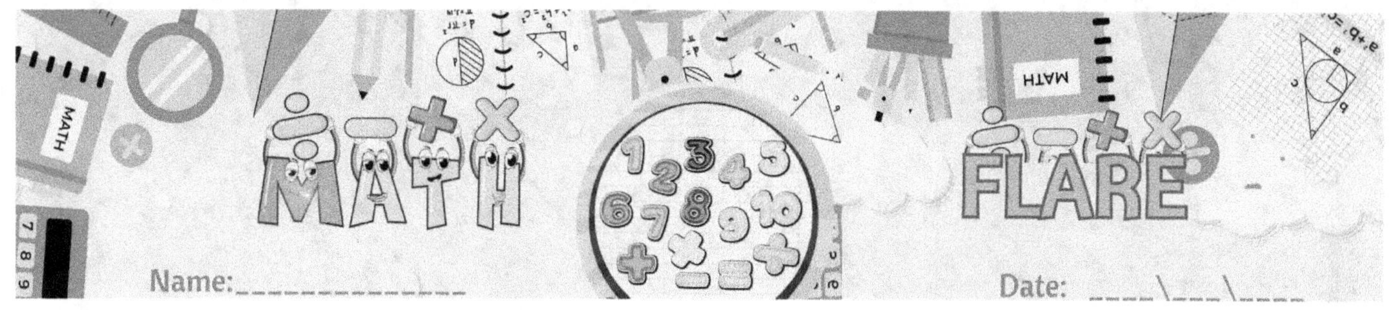

Area and Perimeter

61.

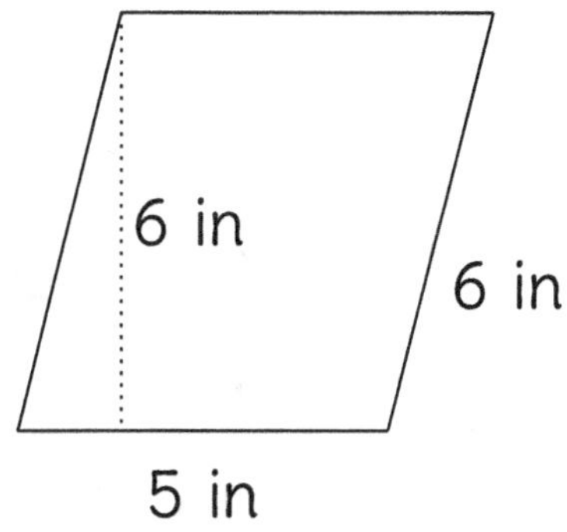

62.

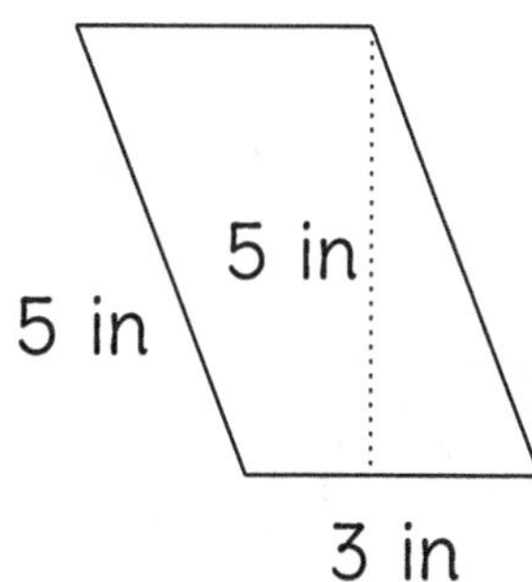

63.

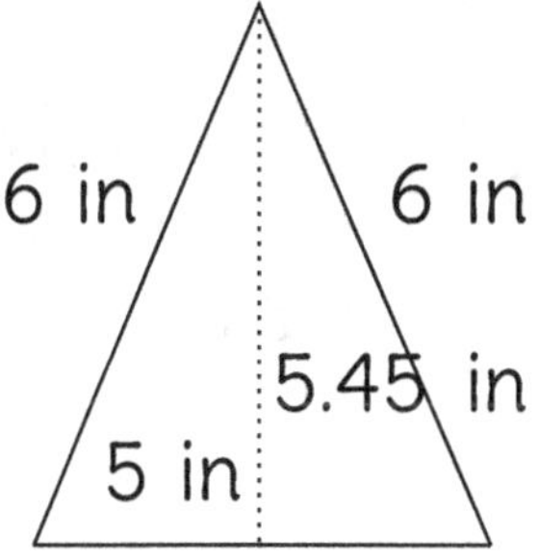

64.

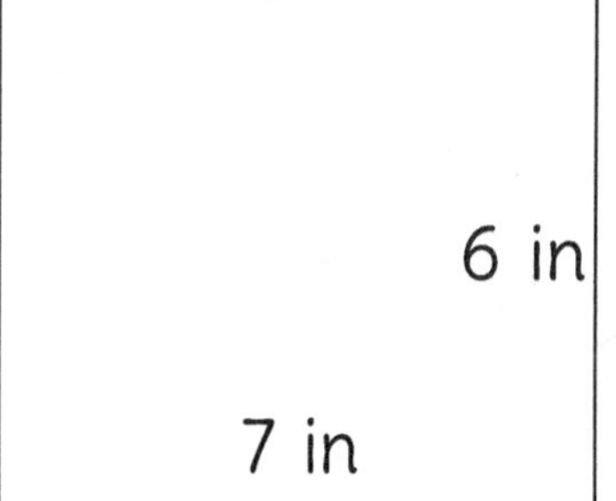

MATH
FLARE
MATH
Name:
Date:

65.

8 in
4 in
8 in
5 in

66.

13 in
7 in
14 in
6 in

67.

3 in
5 in
5 in
5 in
6 in

68.

16 in
16 in
13.856 in
16 in

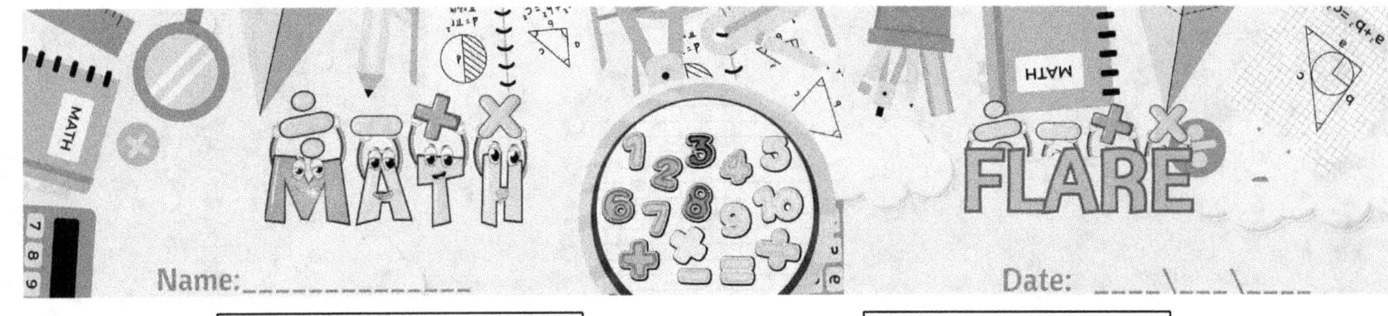

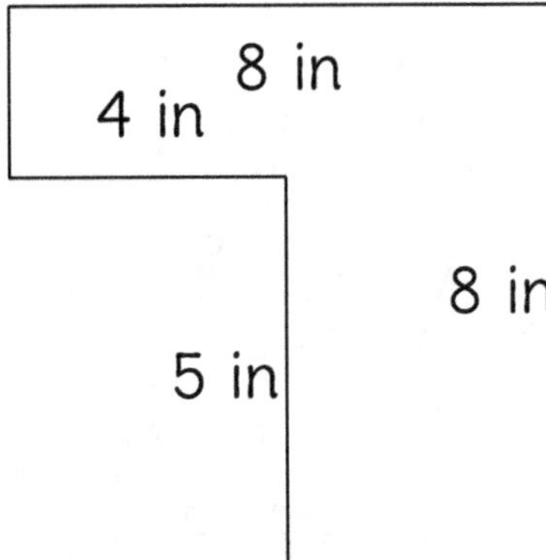

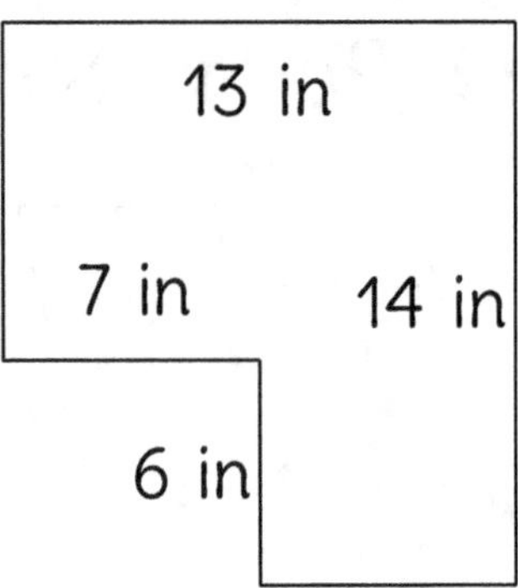

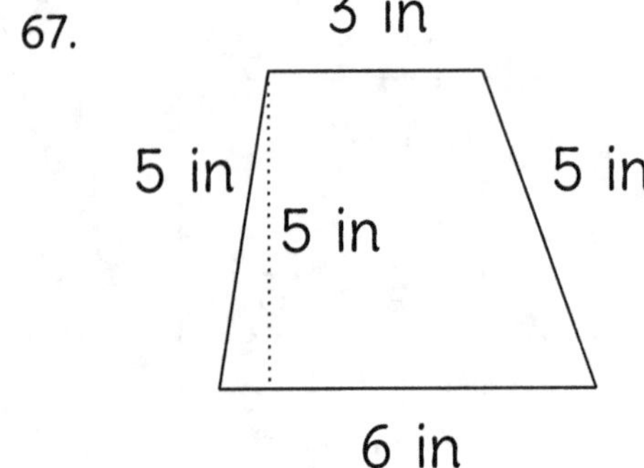

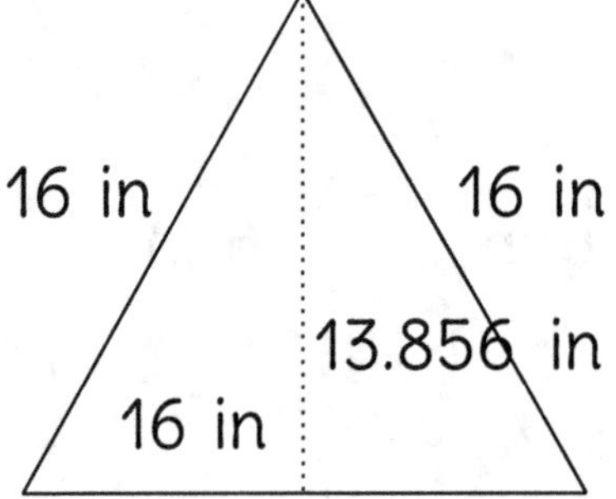

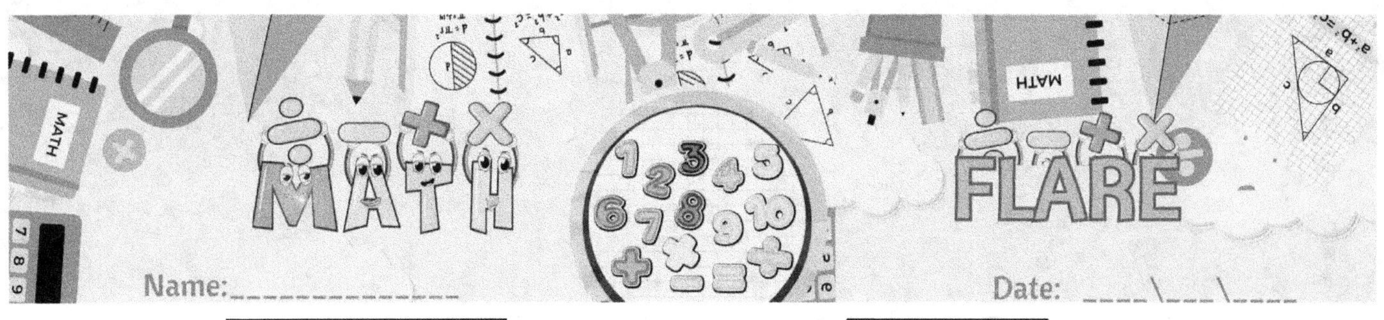

69.

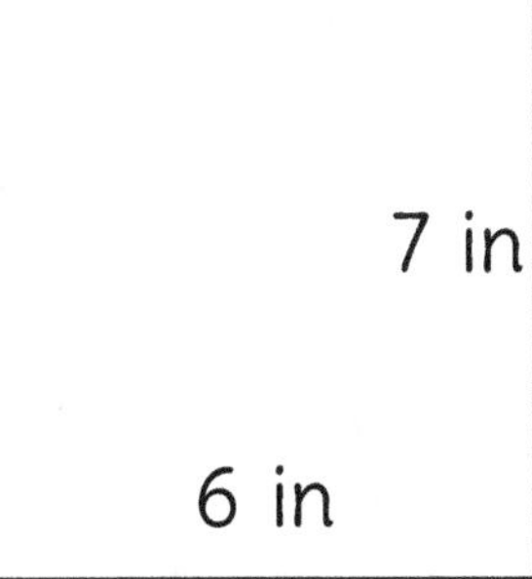

70.

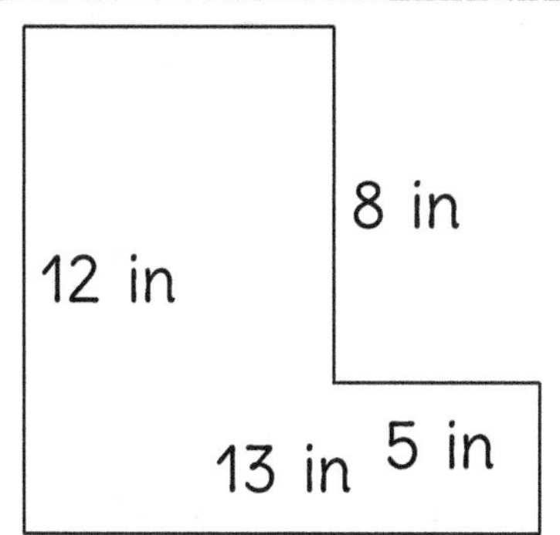

71.

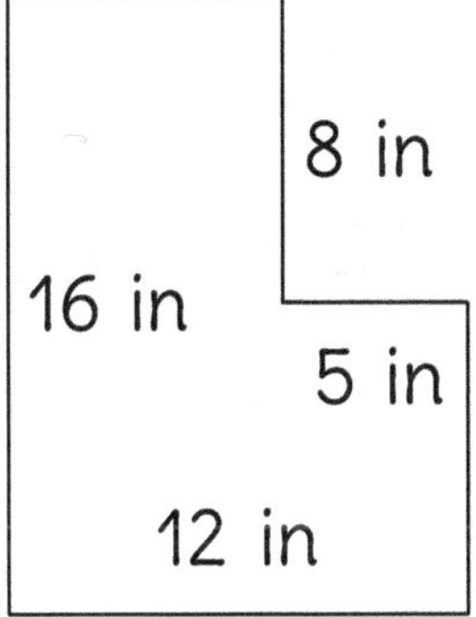

72.

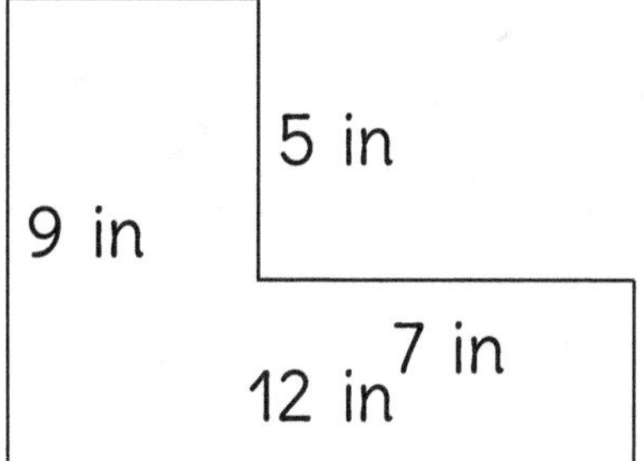

MATH
FLARE
Name:
Date:

73.

10 in
12 in

74.

8 in
7 in

75.

14 in
9 in
10 in

76.

3 in
6 in 2 in
6 in

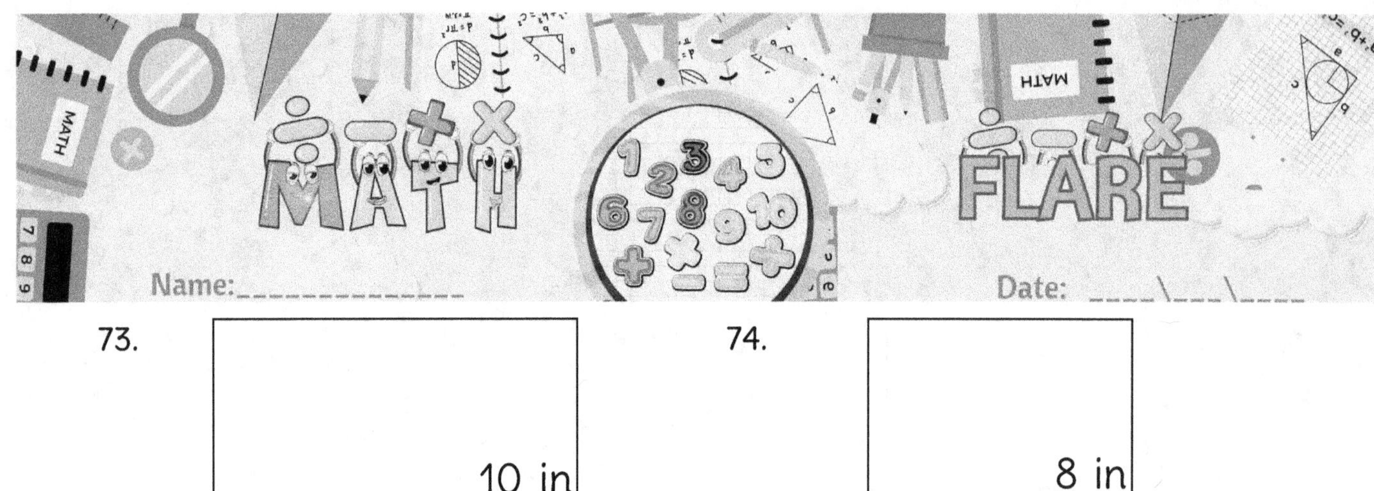

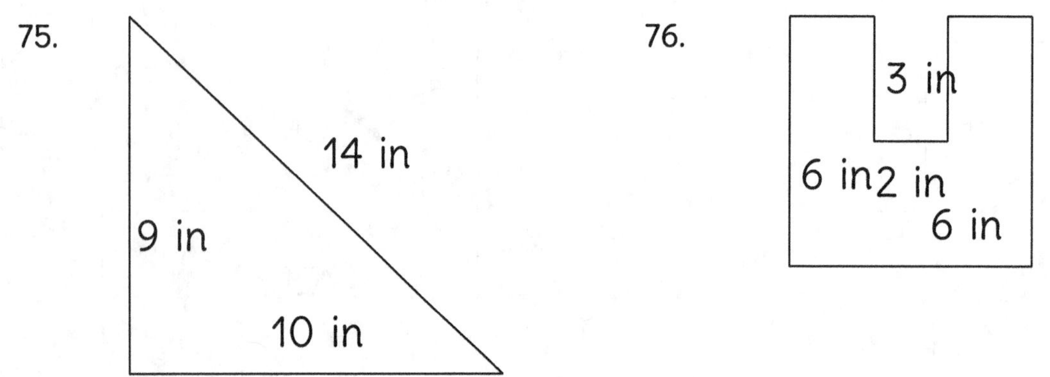

MATH
FLARE
Name:
Date:

77.

11 in
11 in
10.04 in
9 in

78.

6 in
6 in
5.196 in
6 in

79.

12 in
12 in
10.91 in
10 in

80.

20 in
13 in
15 in

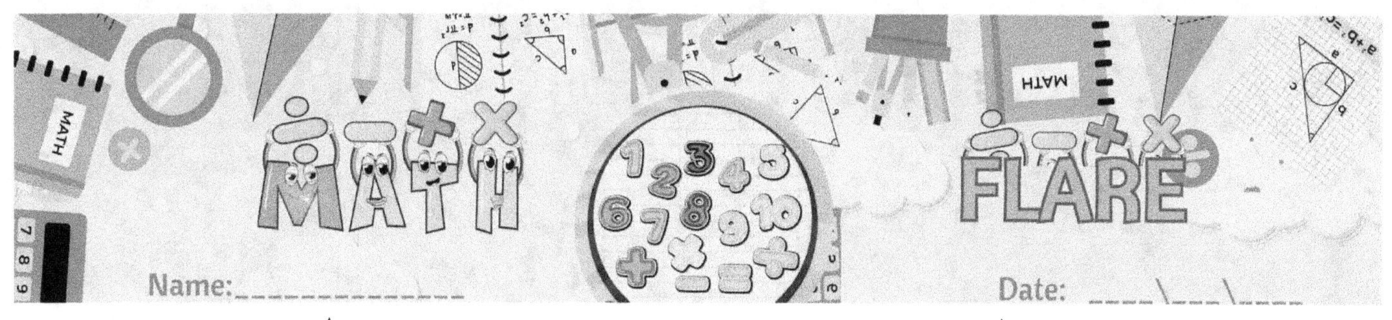

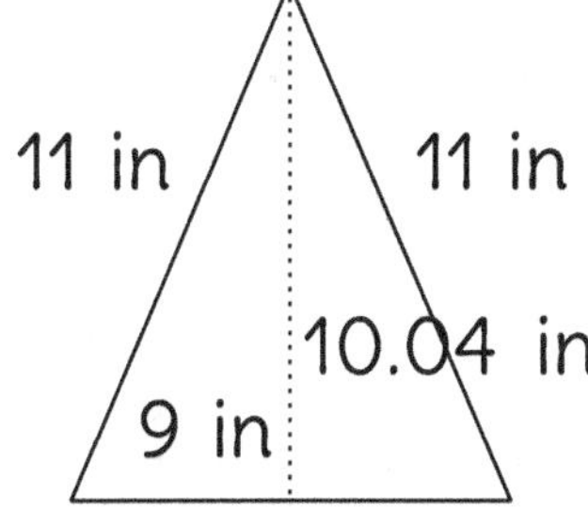

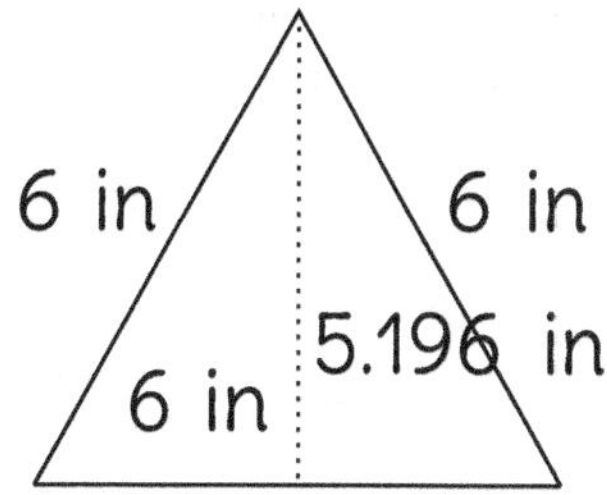

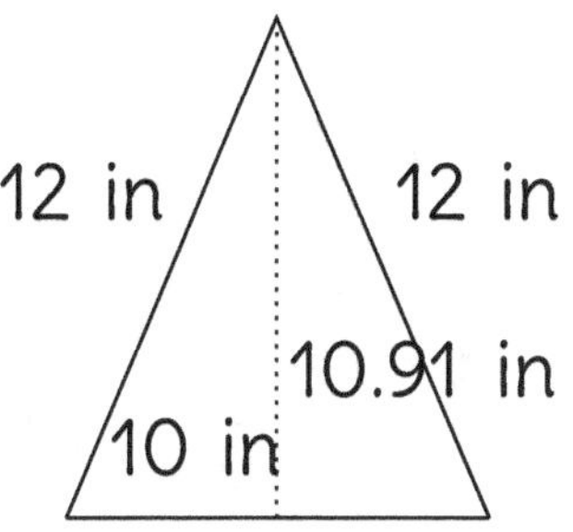

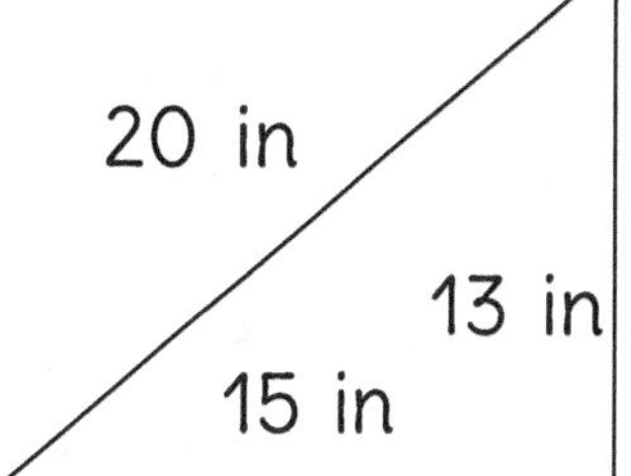

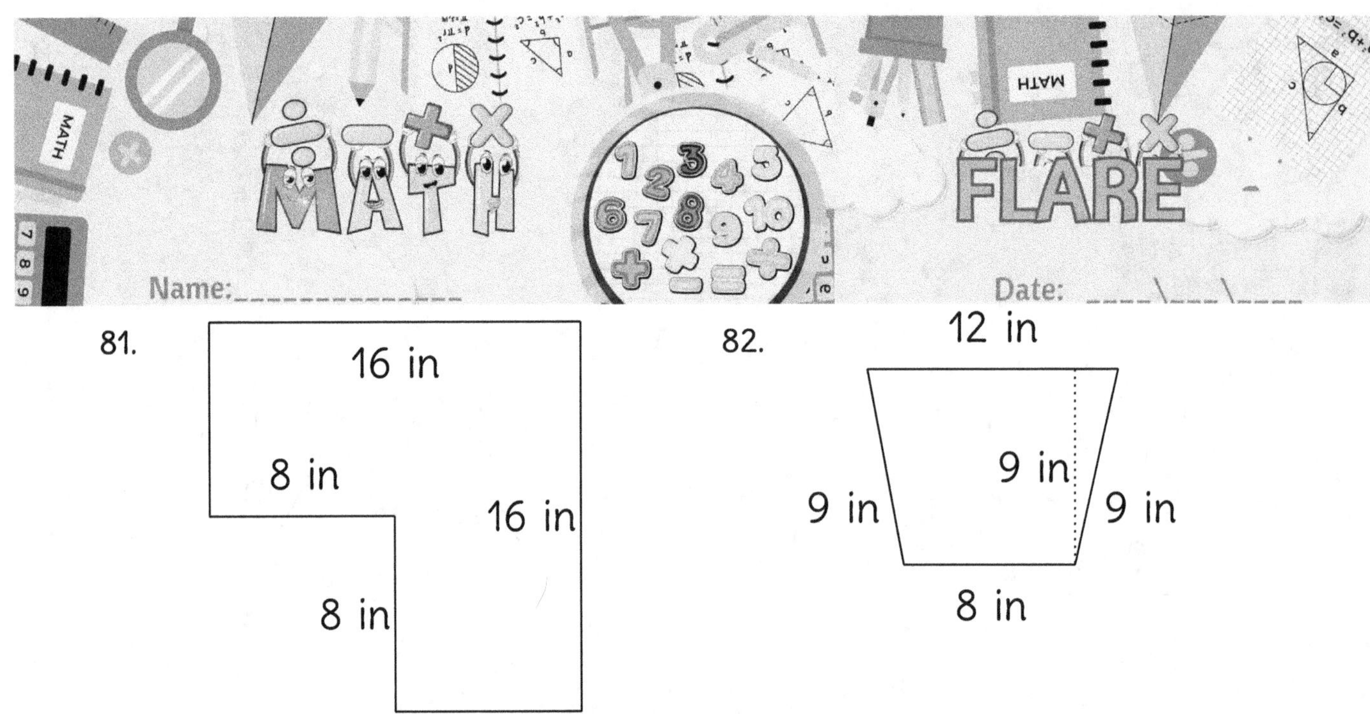

81.

82.

83.

84.

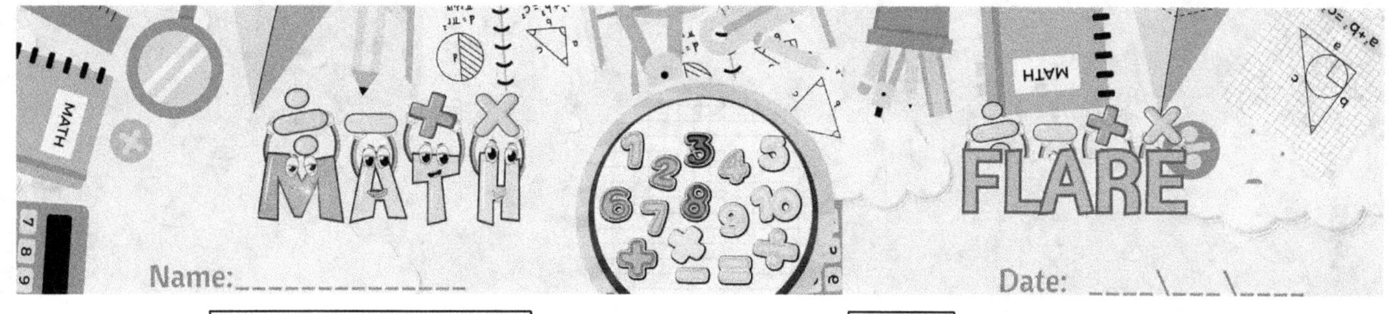

85.

15 in

14 in

15 in

86.

9 in

13 in

9 in

13 in

87.

3 in

10 in

13 in

9 in

88.

17 in

17 in

14.722 in

17 in

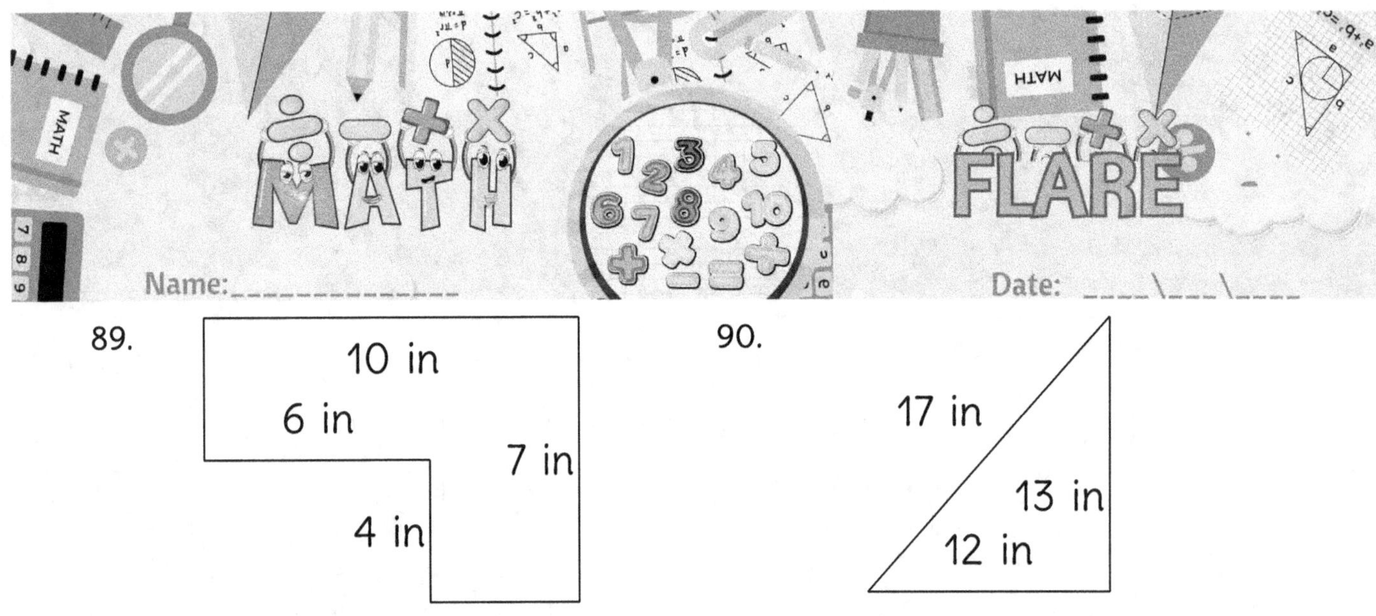

89.

90.

91.

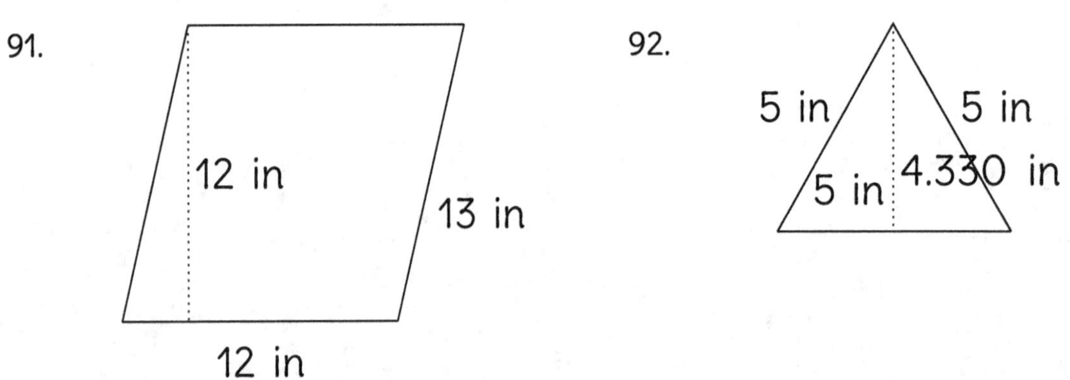

92.

MATH
MATH
FLARE
Name:
Date:

93.

11 in
4 in
9 in
5 in

94.

14 in
14 in
13 in

95.

10 in
8 in
8 in
9 in
16 in

96.

8 in
6 in
6 in

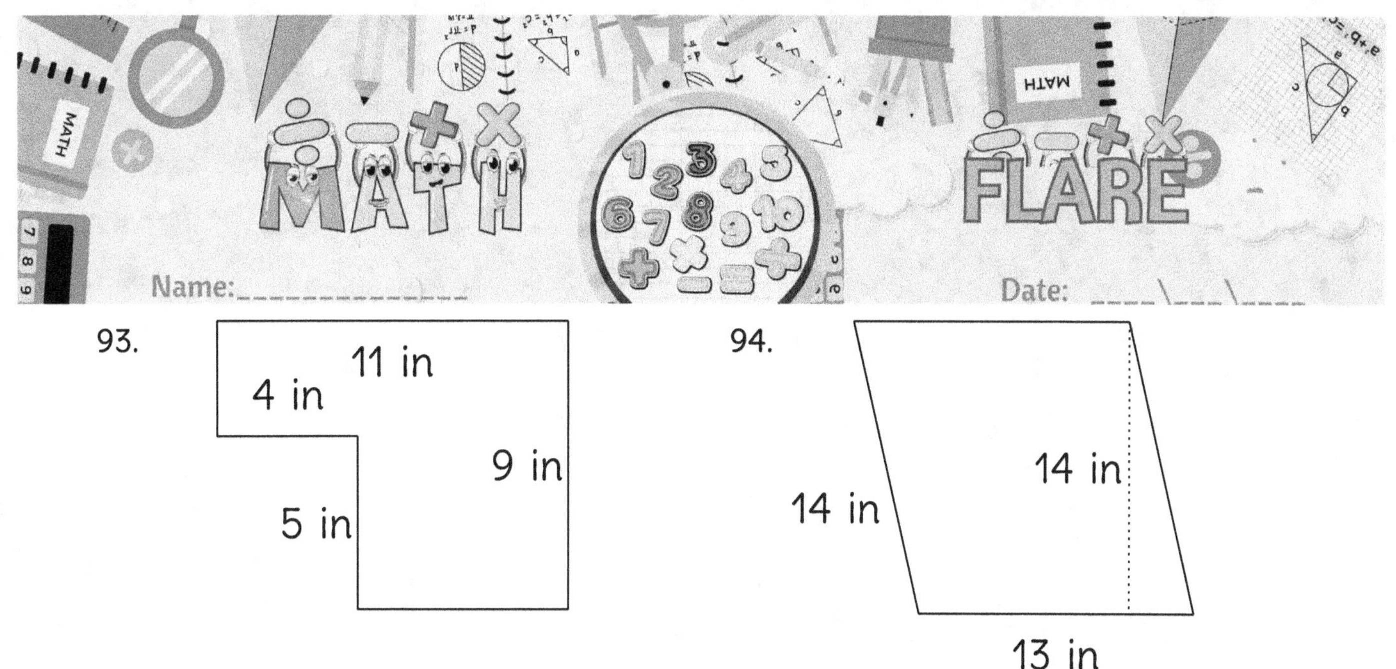

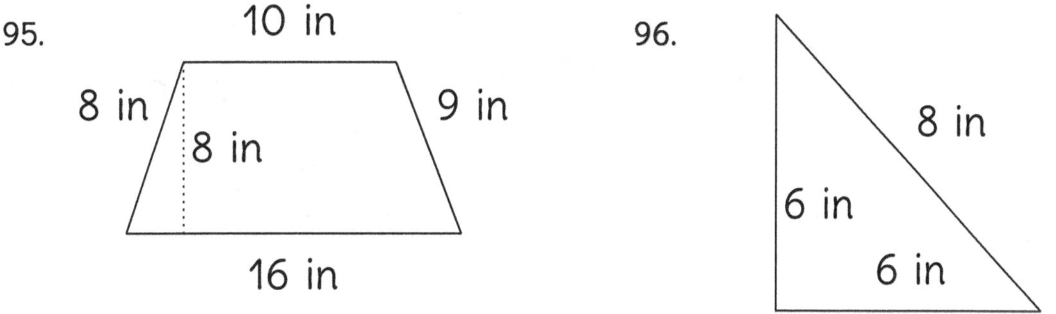

MATH
MATH
FLARE
Name:___________
Date: ____________

97.

18 in
13 in
13 in

98.

12 in
5 in
11 in
5 in

99.

18 in
16 in

100.

6 in
11 in
5.52 in
12 in

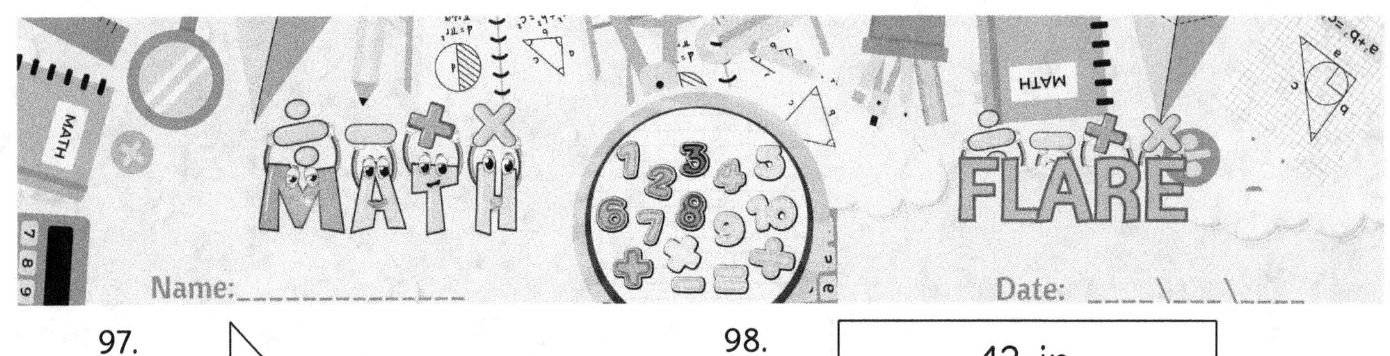

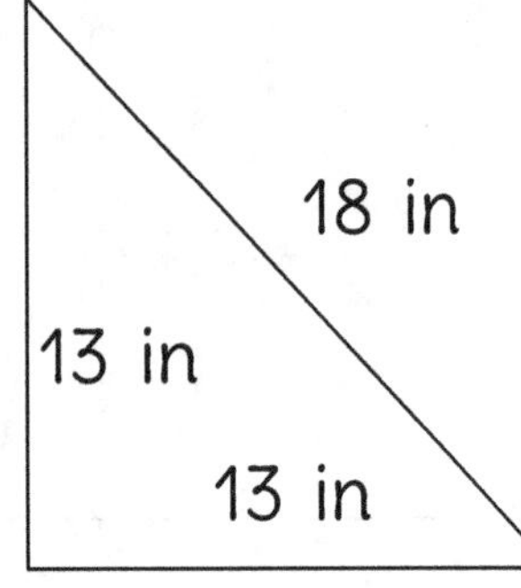

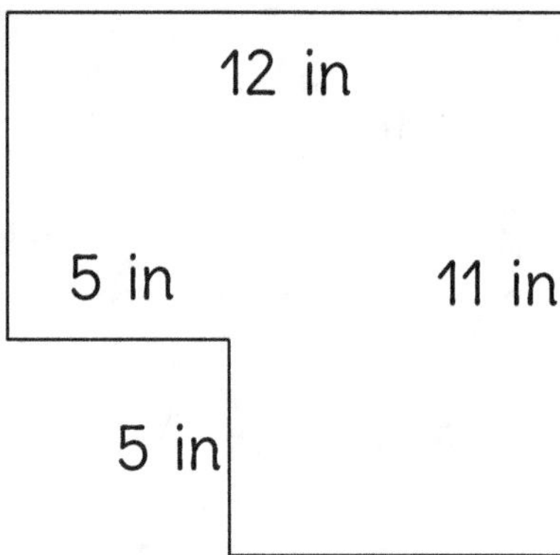

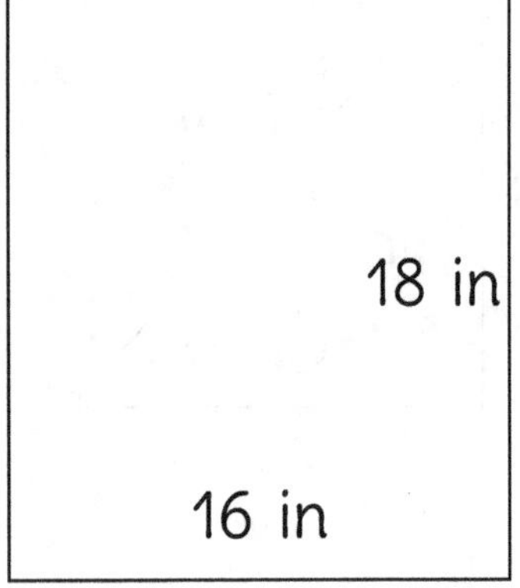

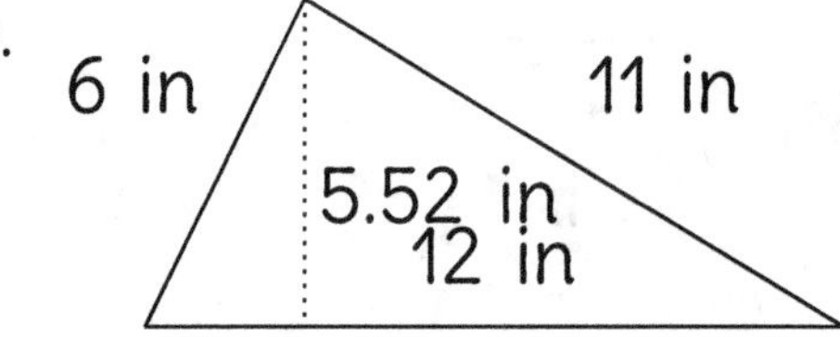

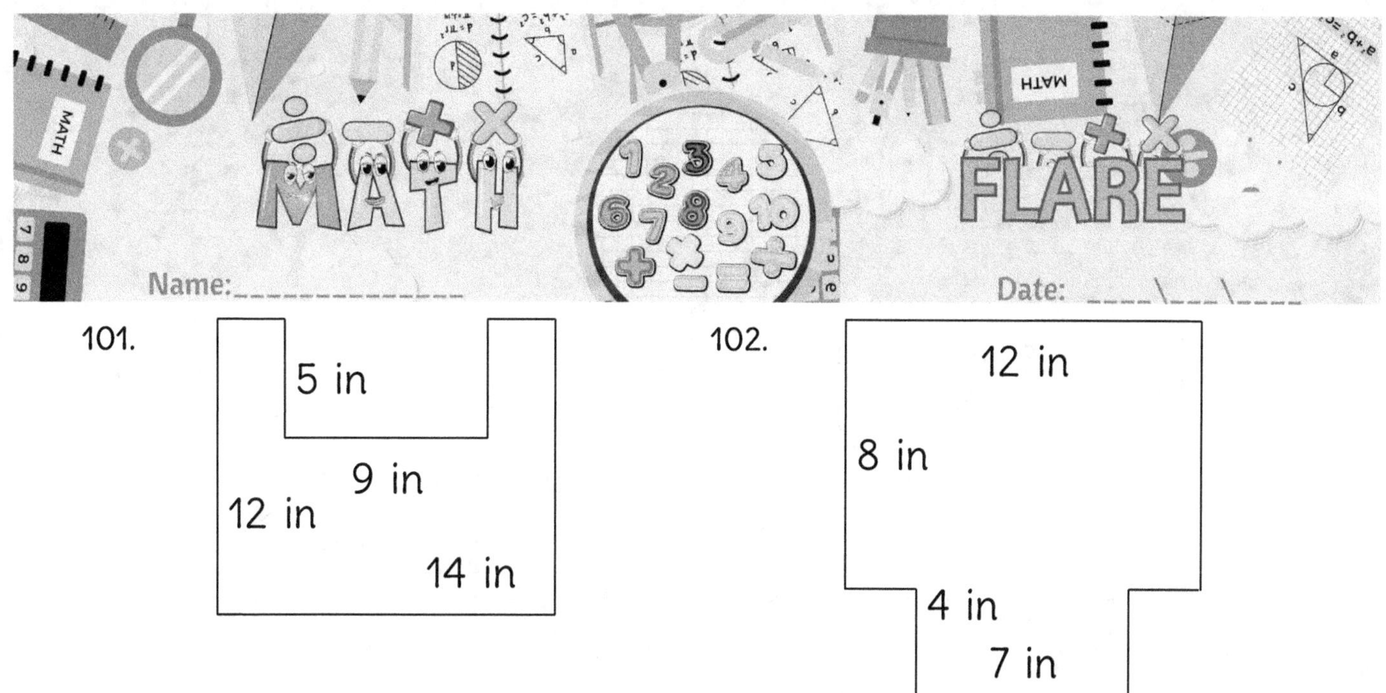

101.
5 in
9 in
12 in
14 in

102.
12 in
8 in
4 in
7 in

103.
15 in
15 in

104.
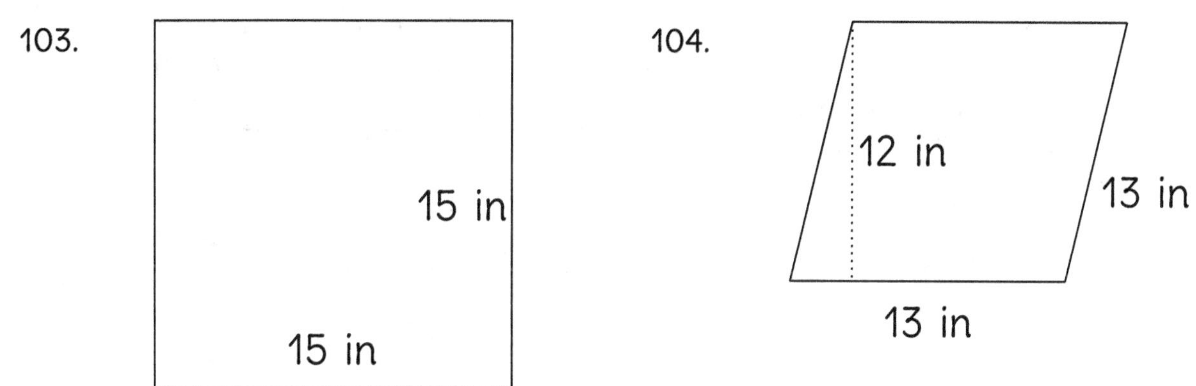

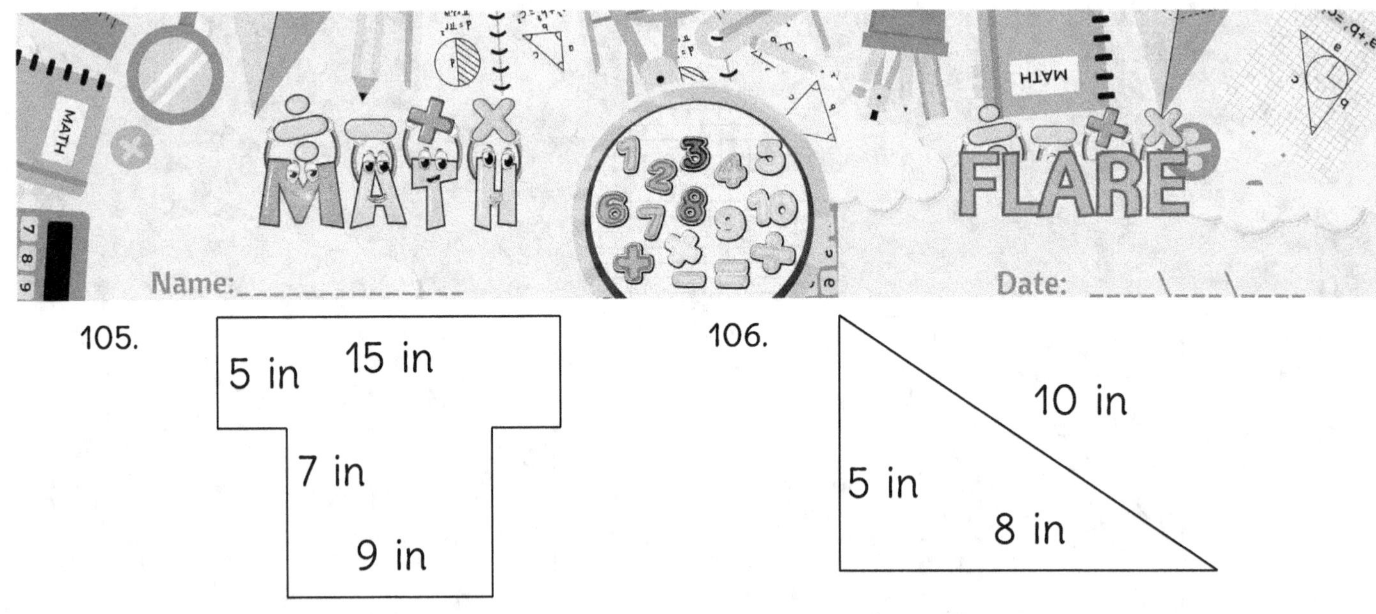

105.

106.

107.

108.

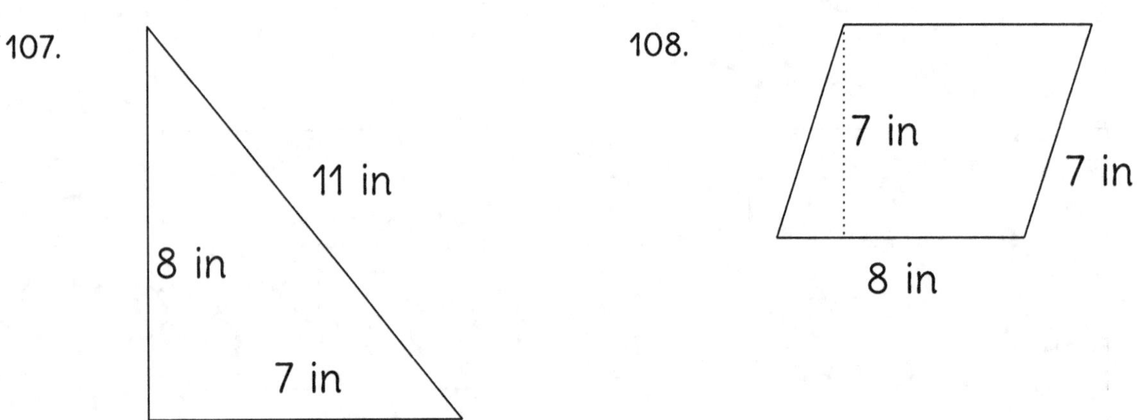

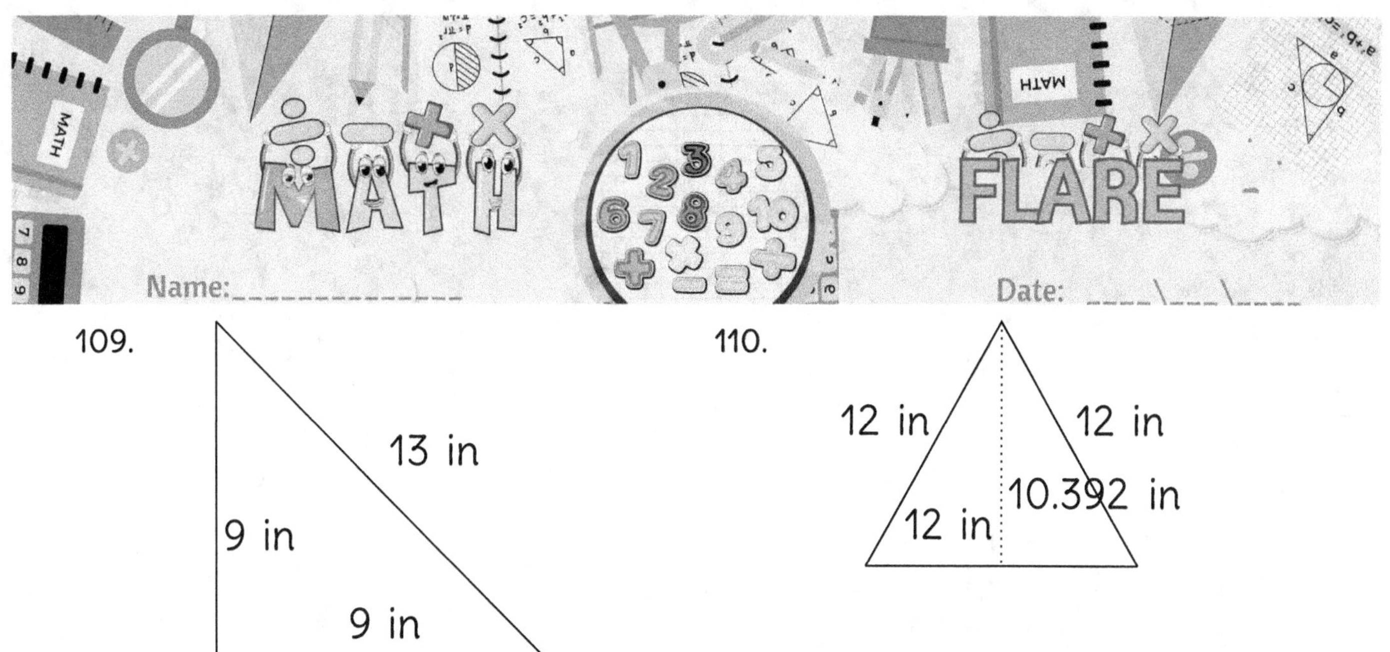

109.

110.

111.
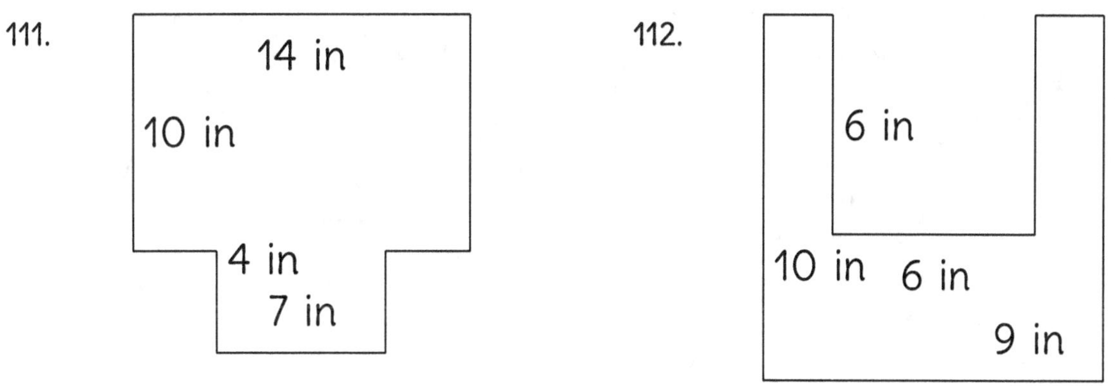

112.

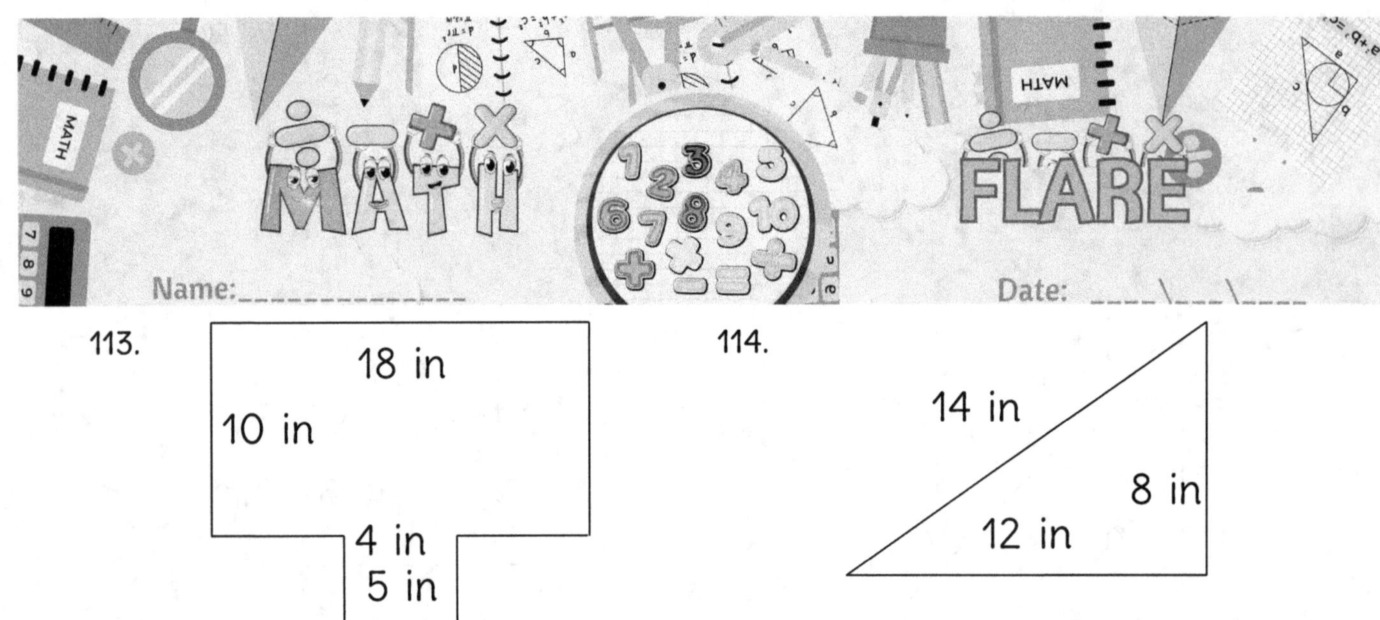

113.

114.

115.

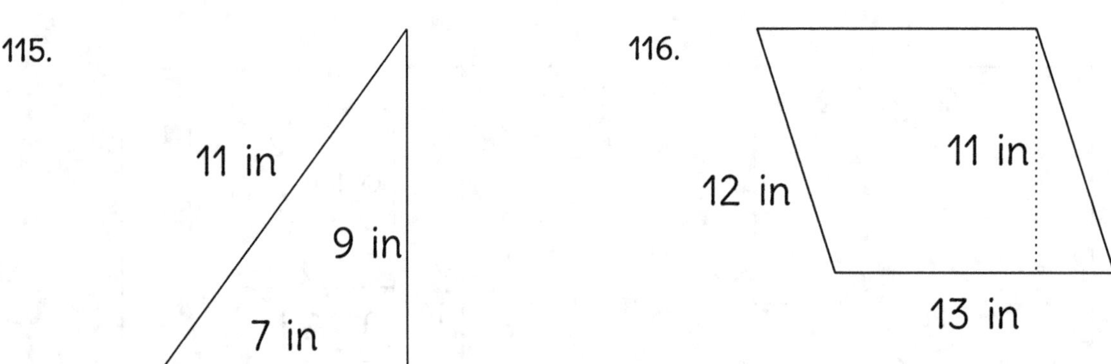

116.

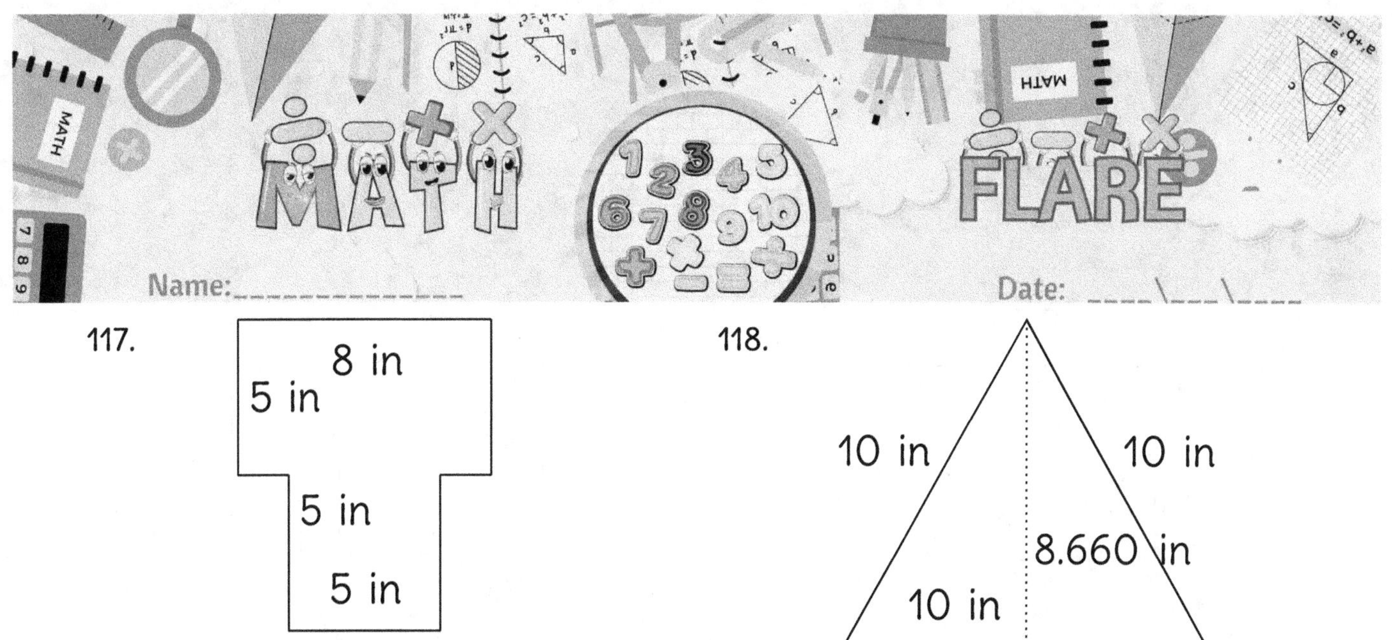

117.

118.

119.

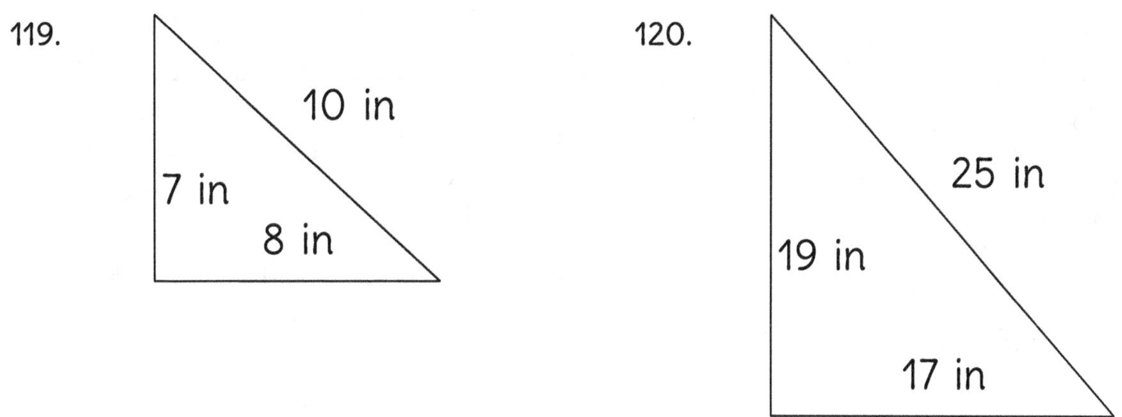

120.

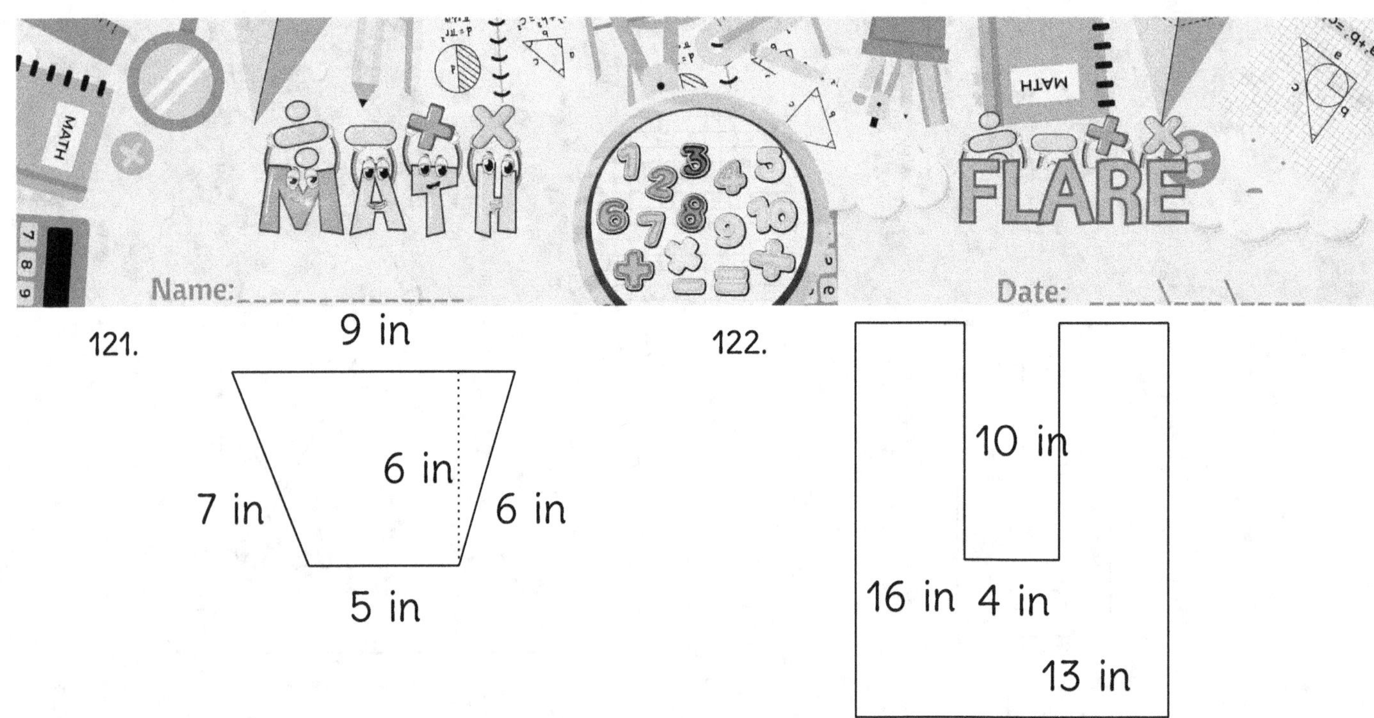

121.

122.

123.

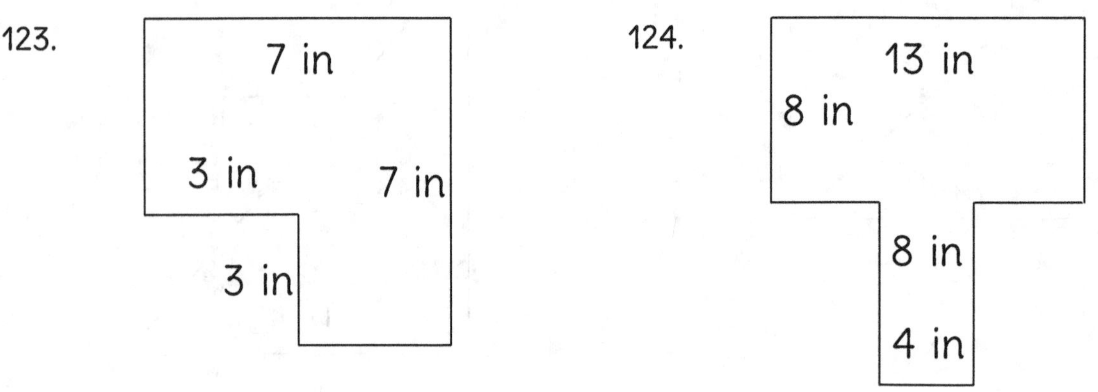

124.

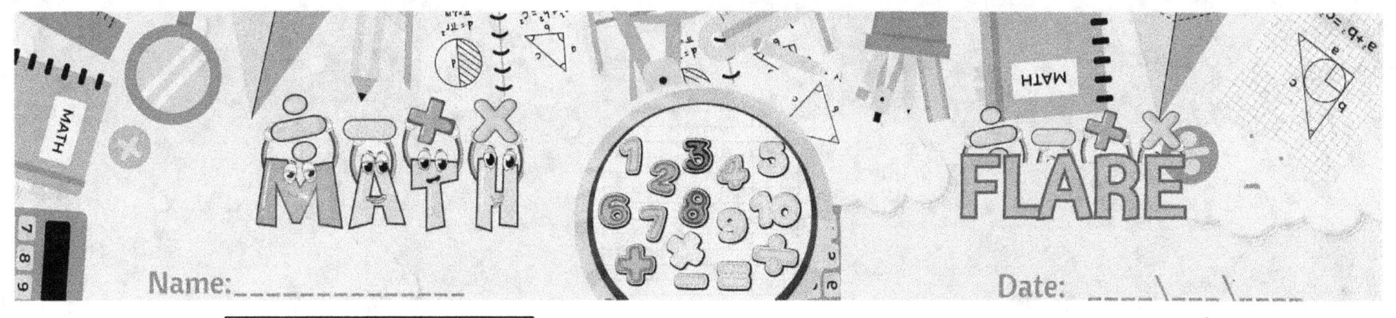

125.

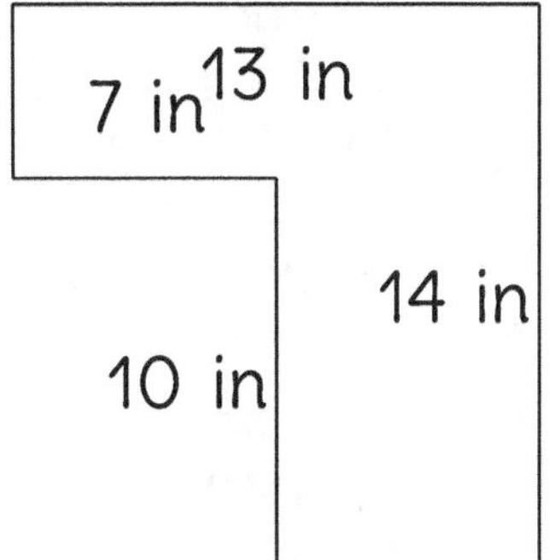

126.

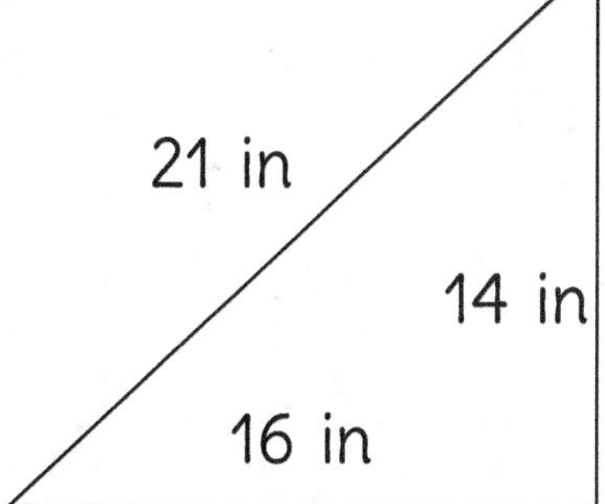

127.

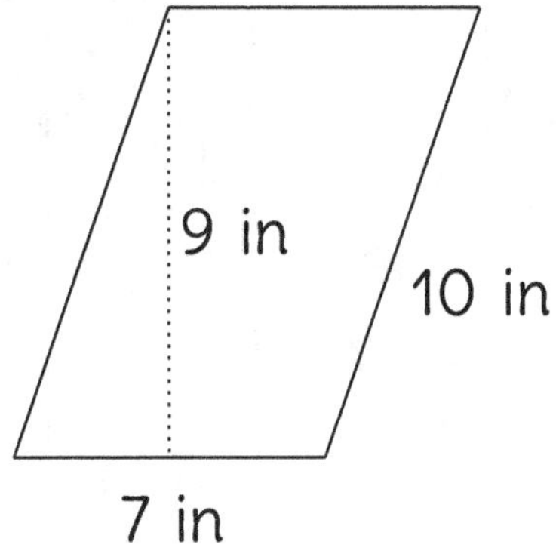

128.

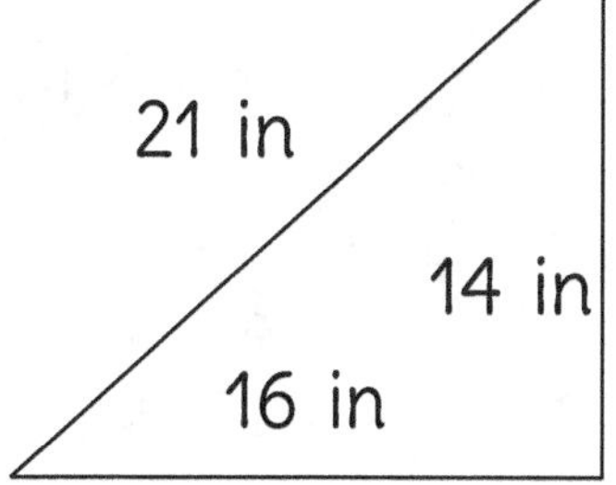

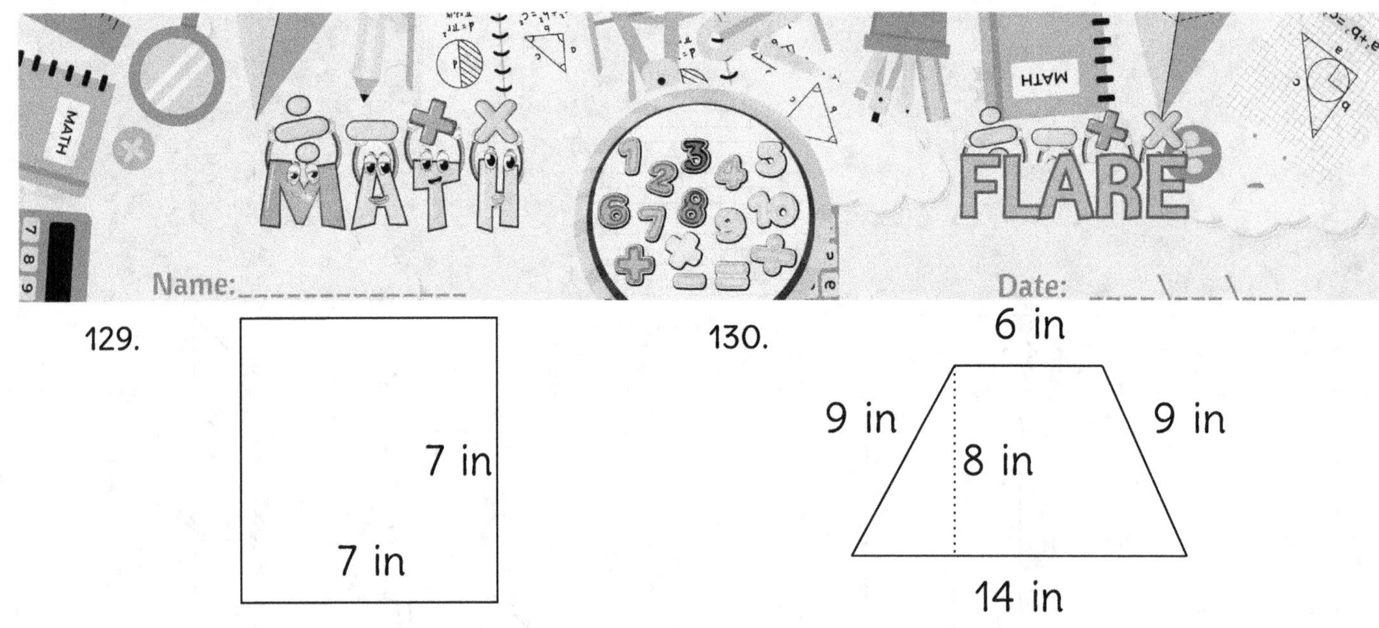

129.

130.

131.

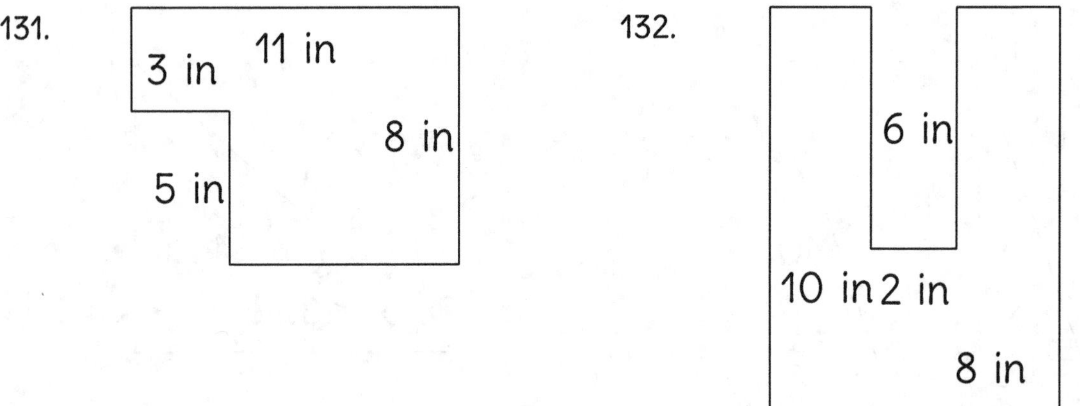

132.

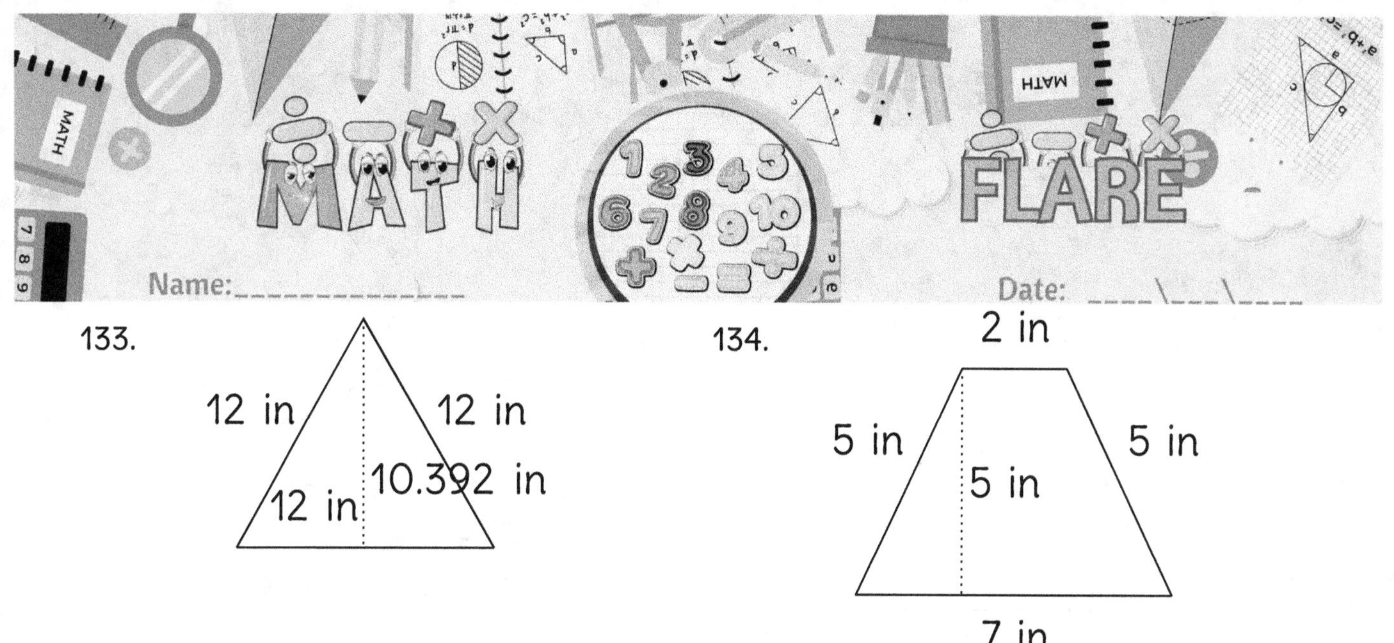

133.

134.

135.
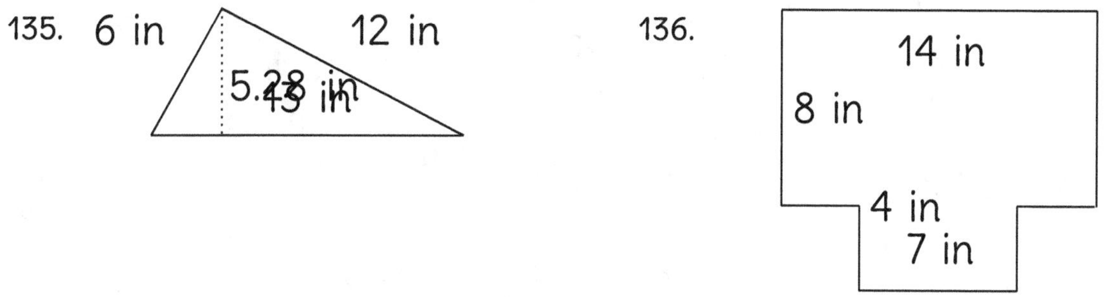

136.

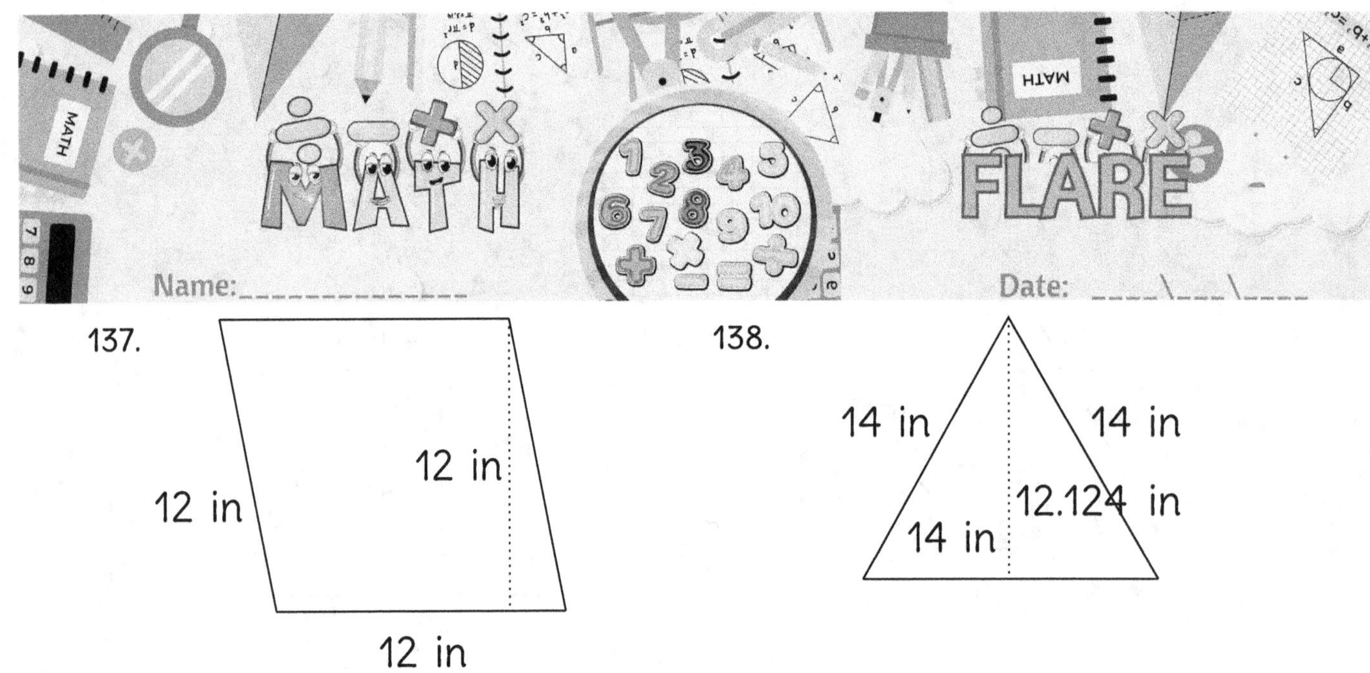

137.

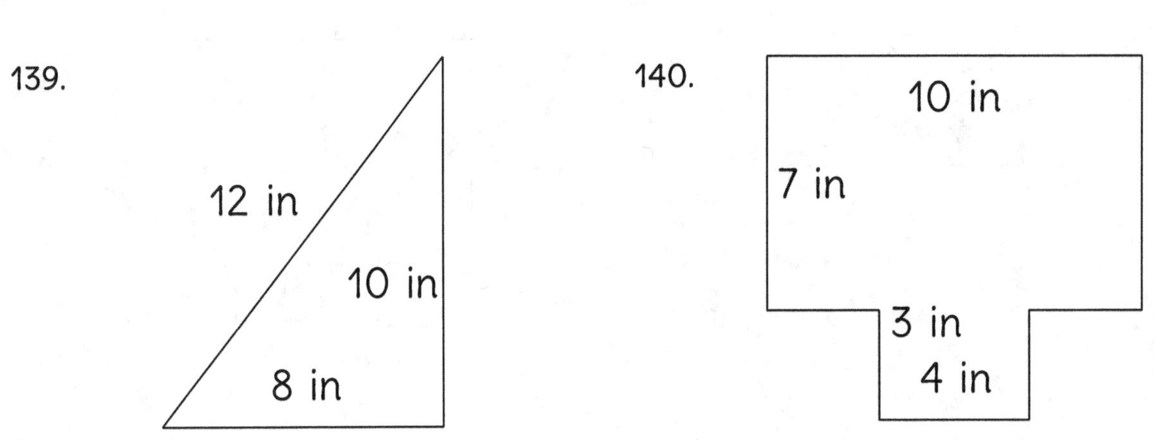

138.

139.

140.

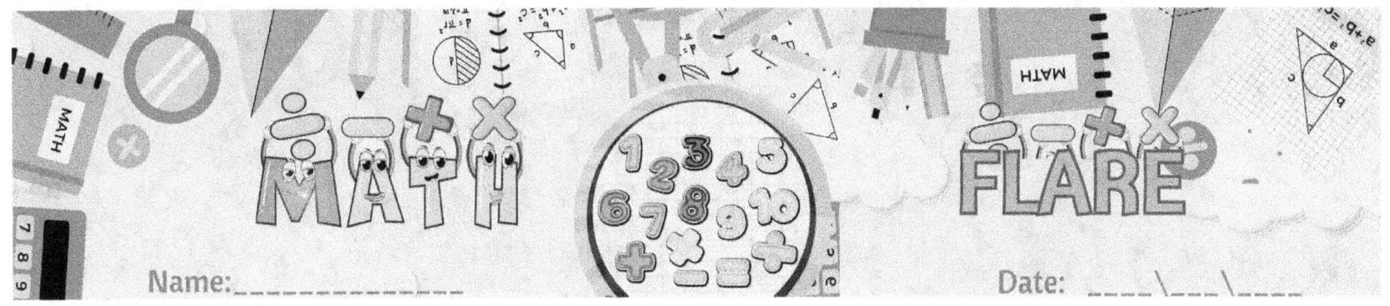

Volume and Surface Area

141.
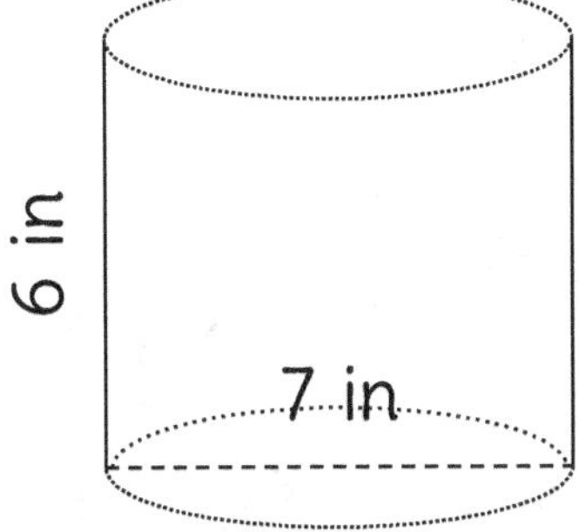

142.
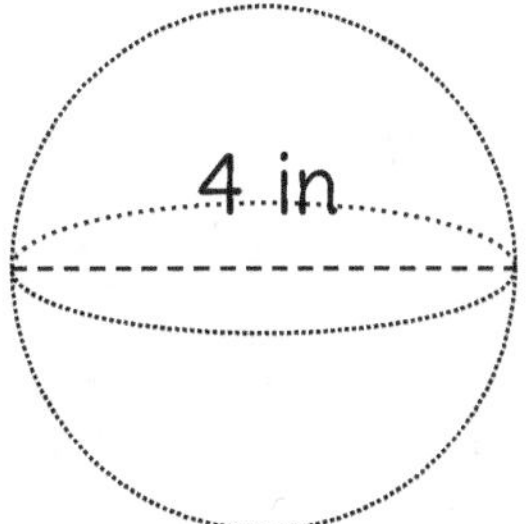

143.
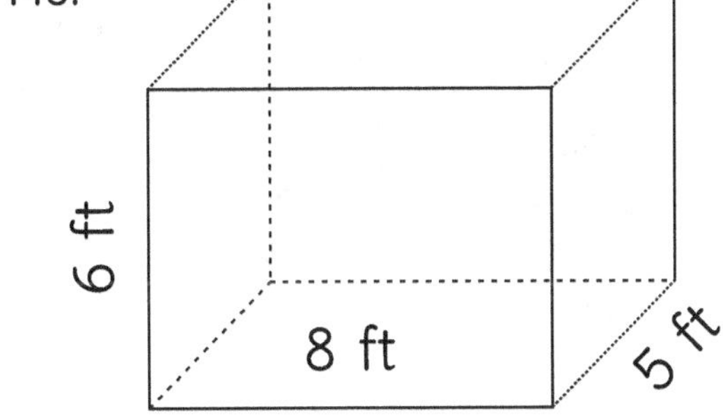

144.
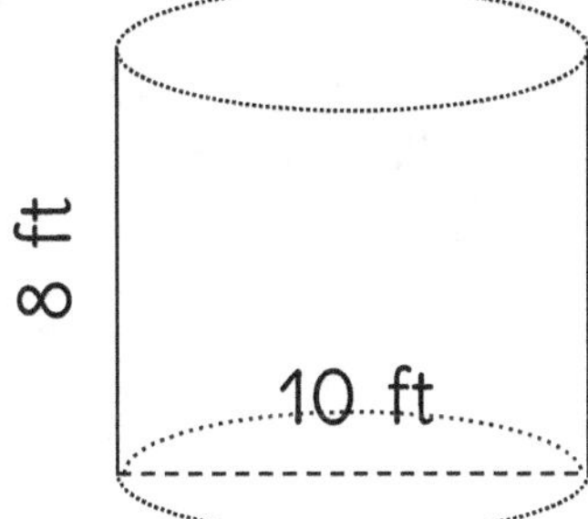

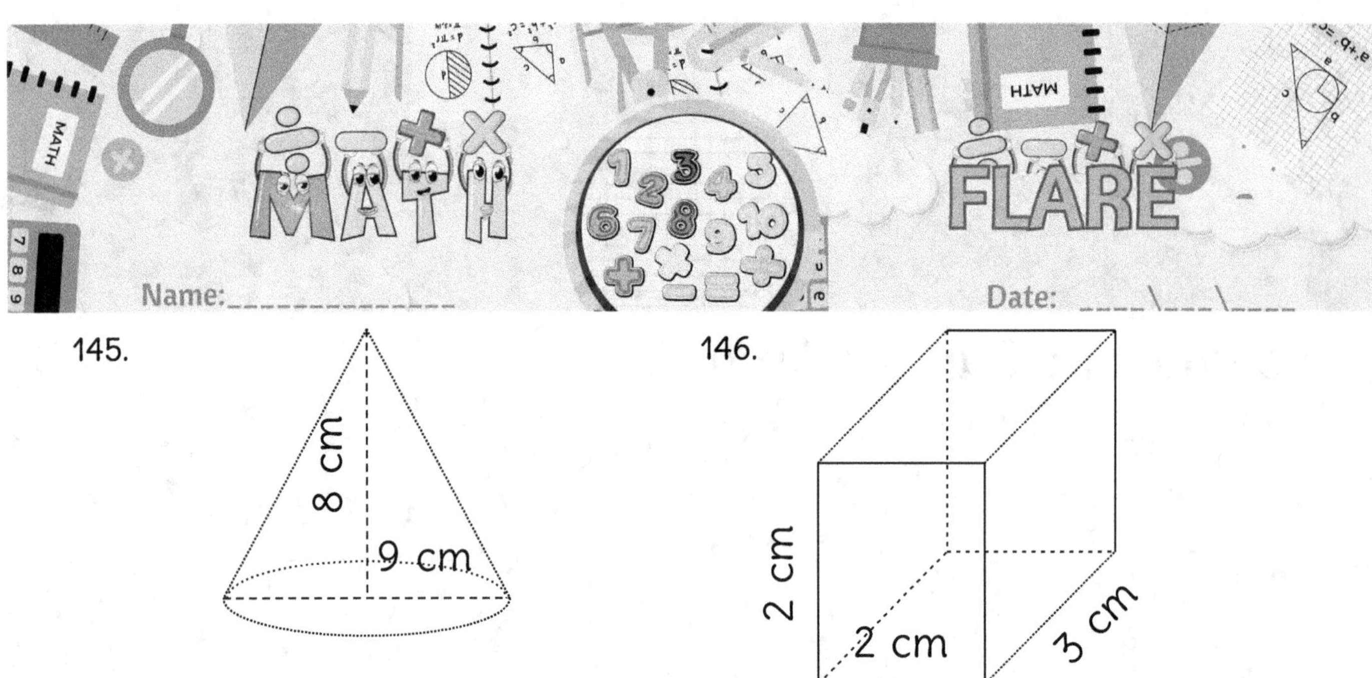

145.

146.

147.

148.

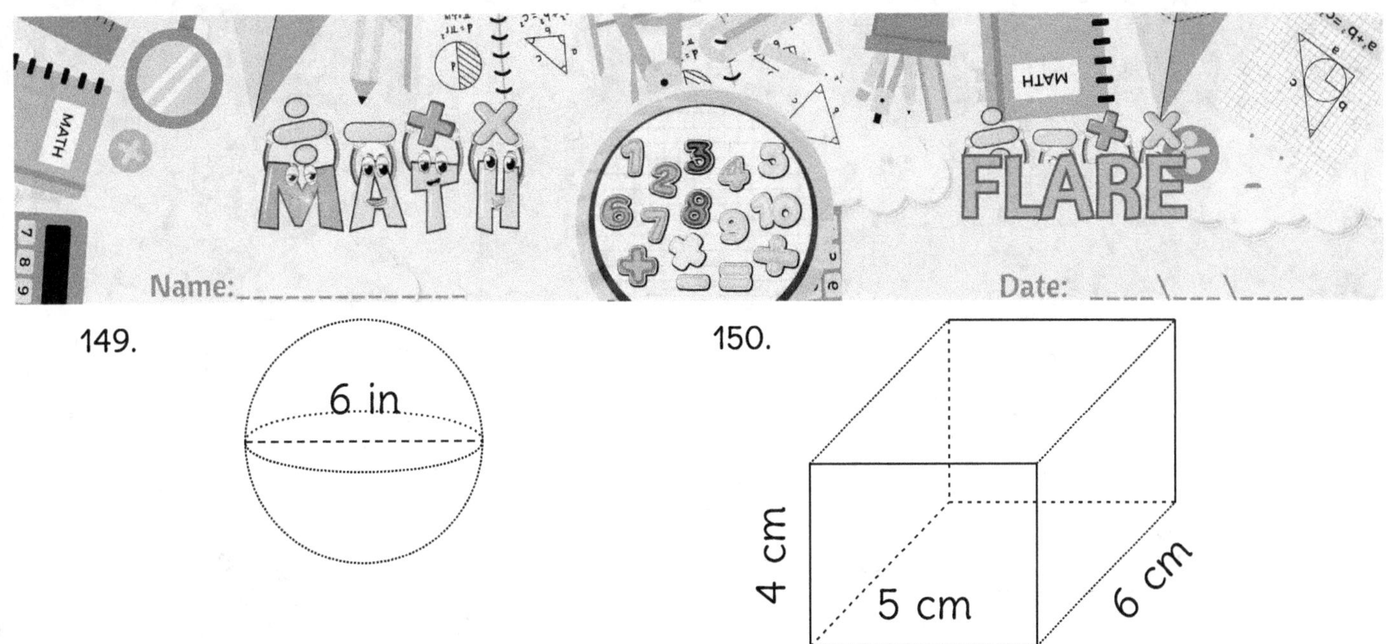

149.

150.

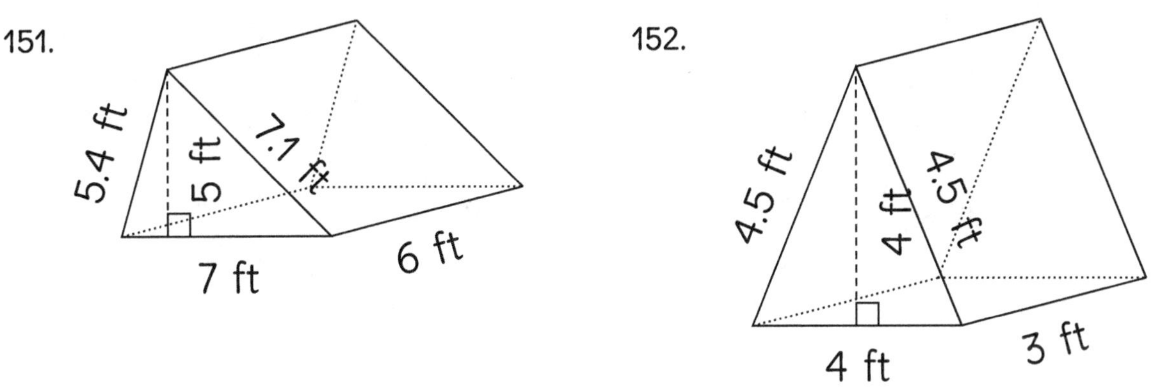

151.

152.

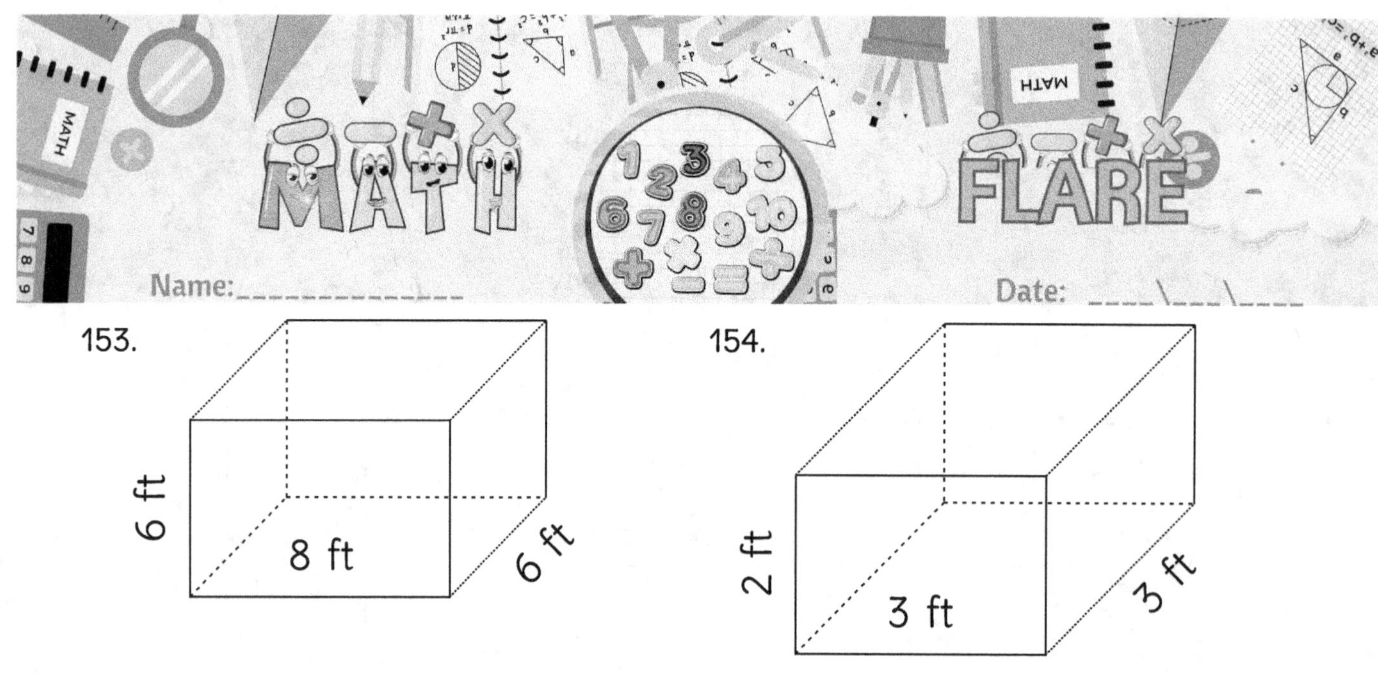

153.

154.

155.
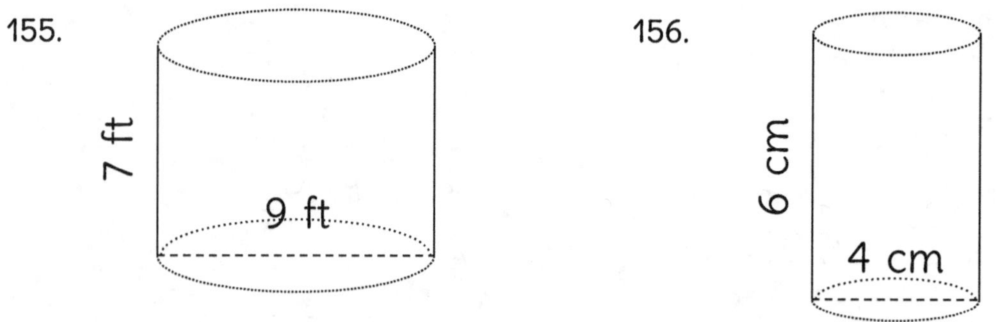

156.

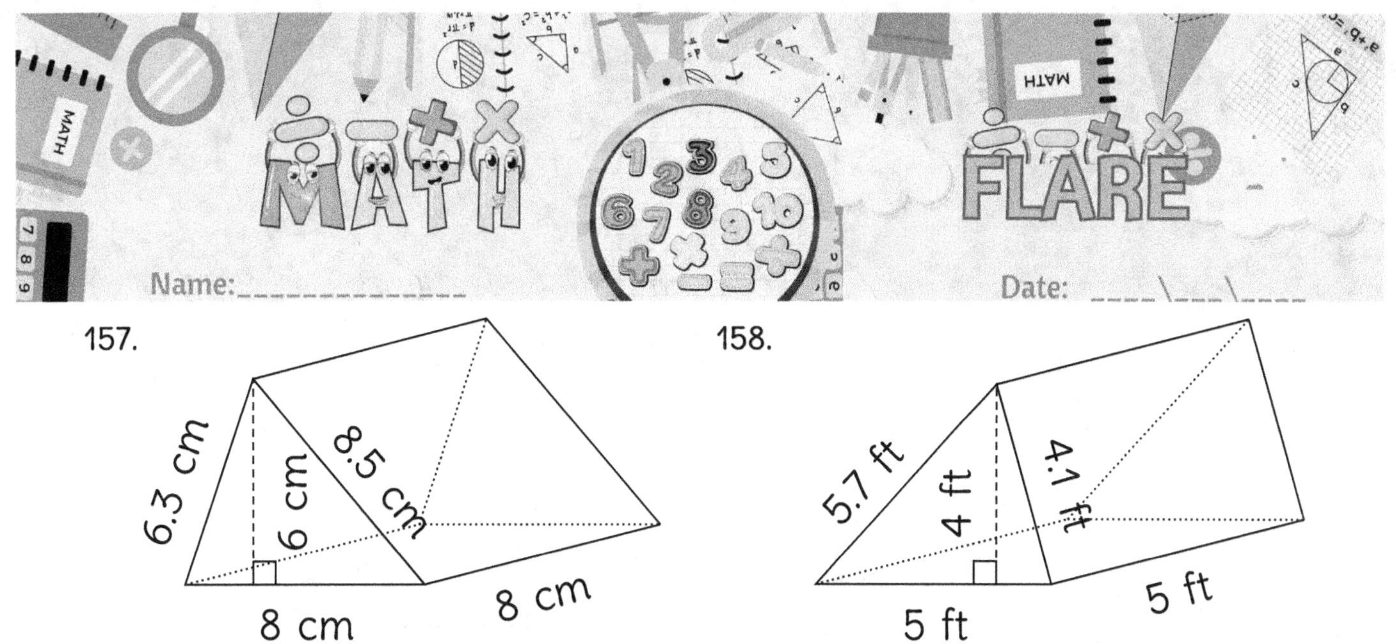
157.
6.3 cm
6 cm
8.5 cm
8 cm
8 cm
158.
5.7 ft
4 ft
4.1 ft
5 ft
5 ft

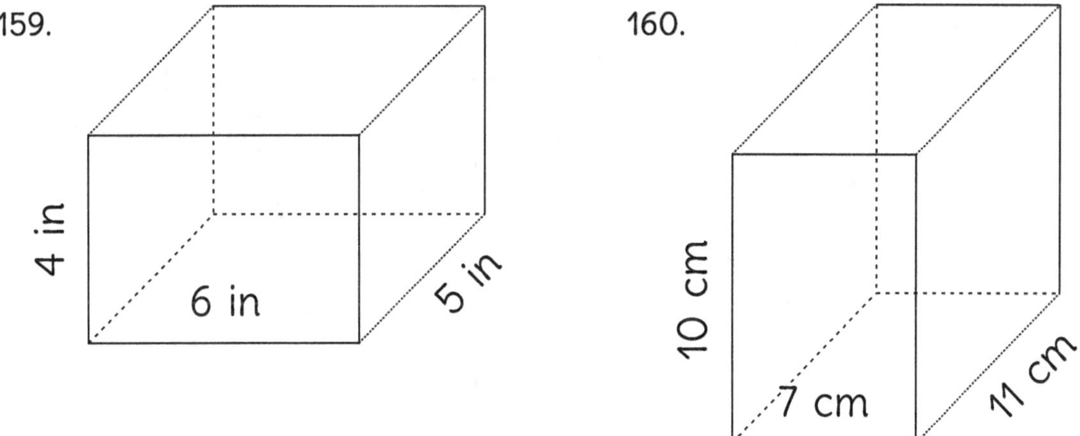
159.
4 in
6 in
5 in
160.
10 cm
7 cm
11 cm

161.

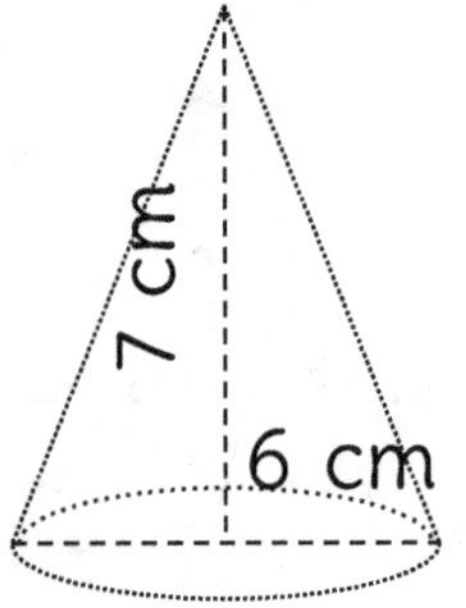

162.

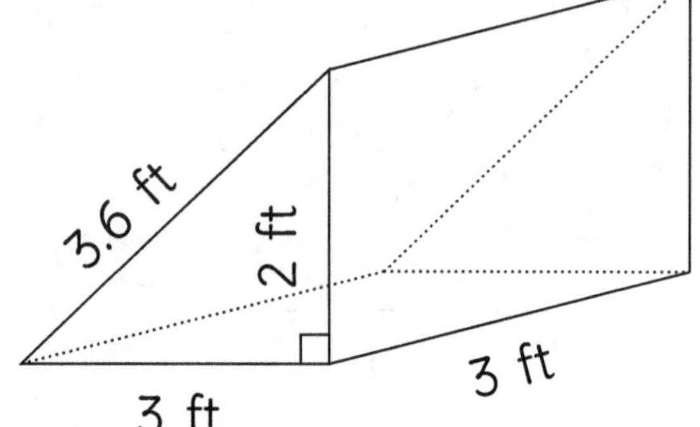

163.

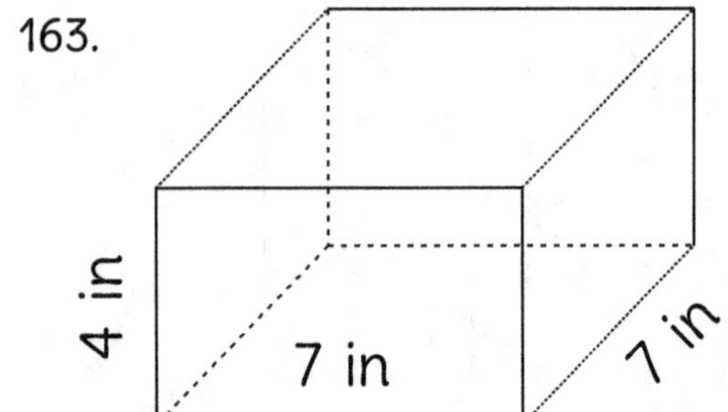

164.

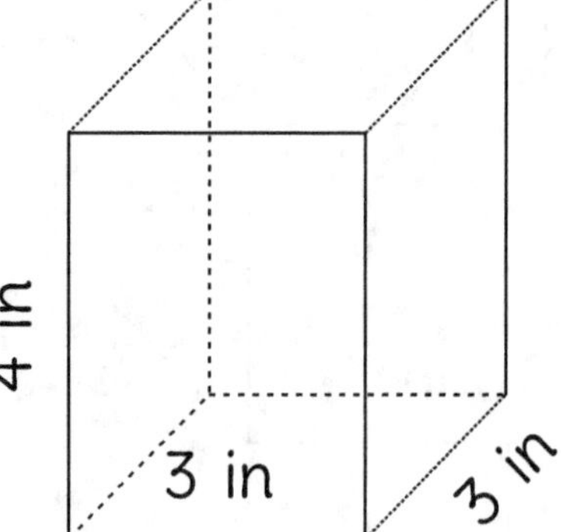

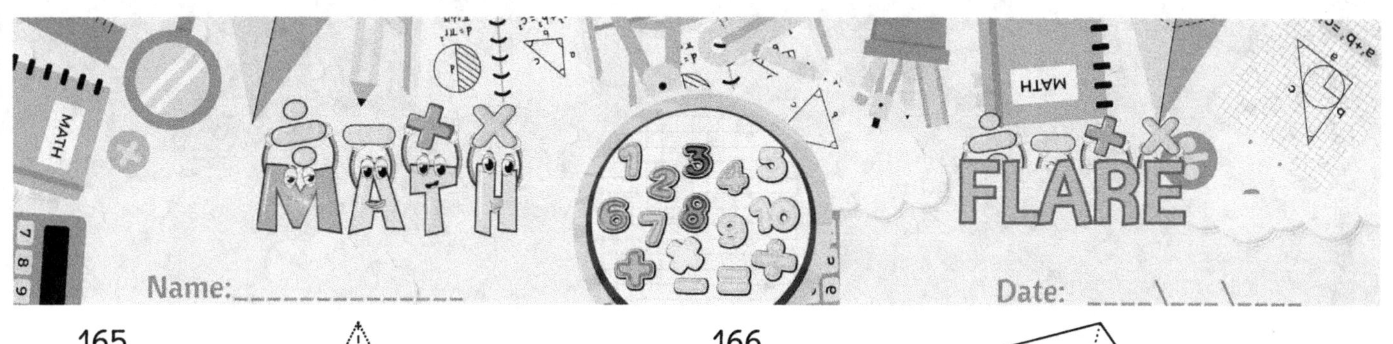

165.

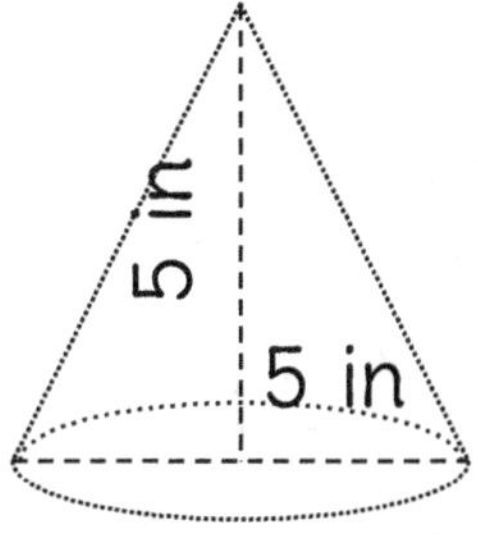

166.

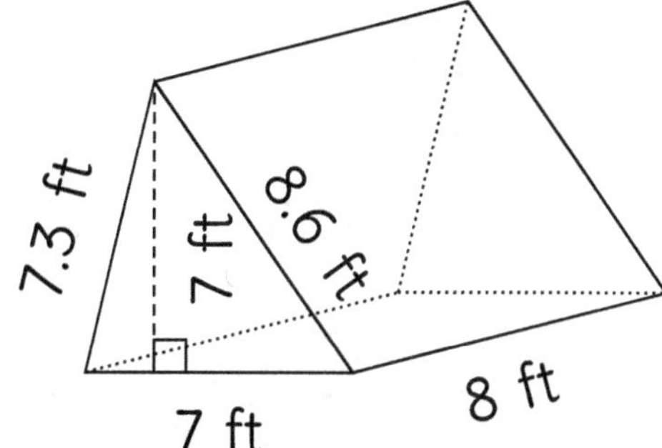

167.

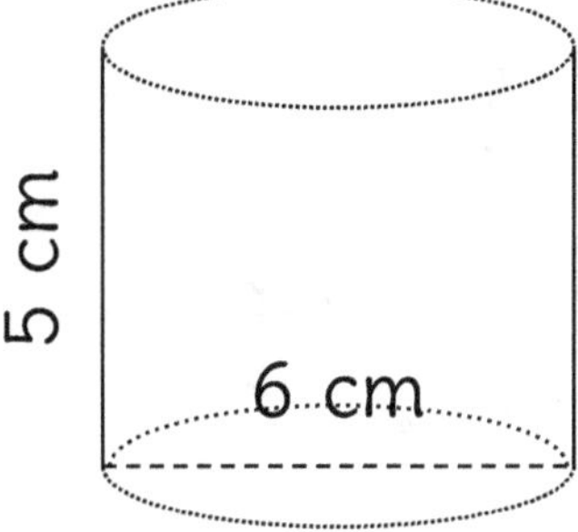

168.

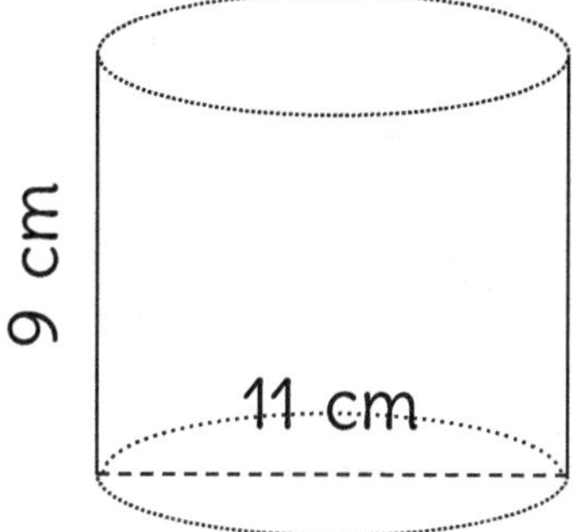

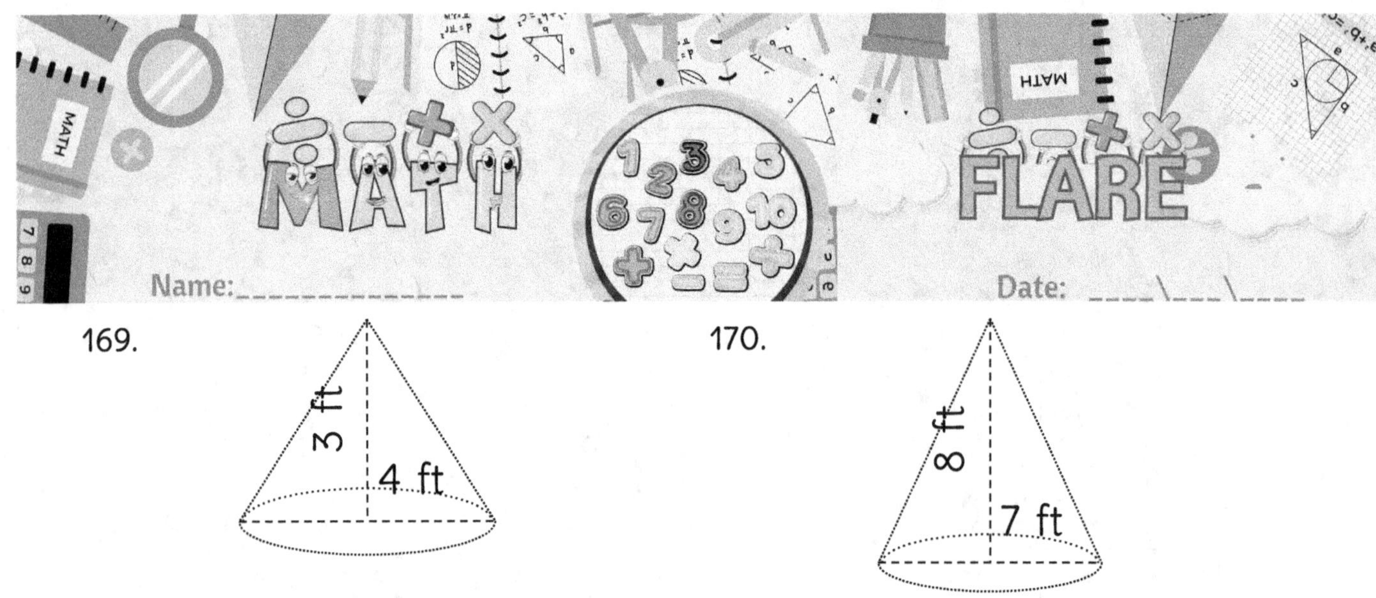

169.

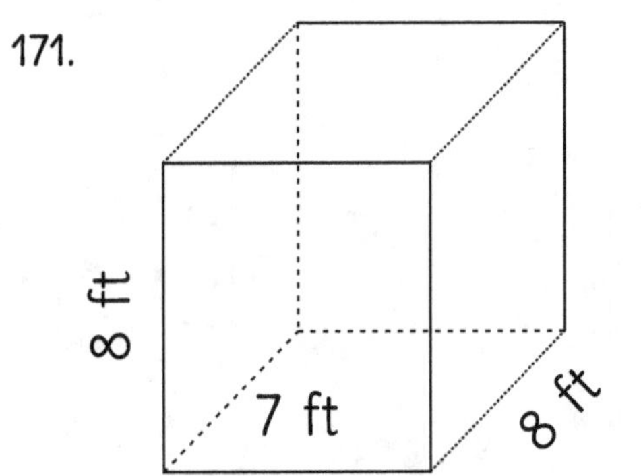

170.

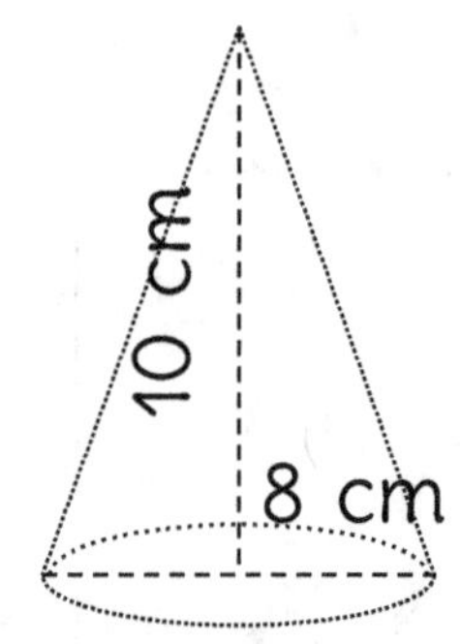

171.

172.

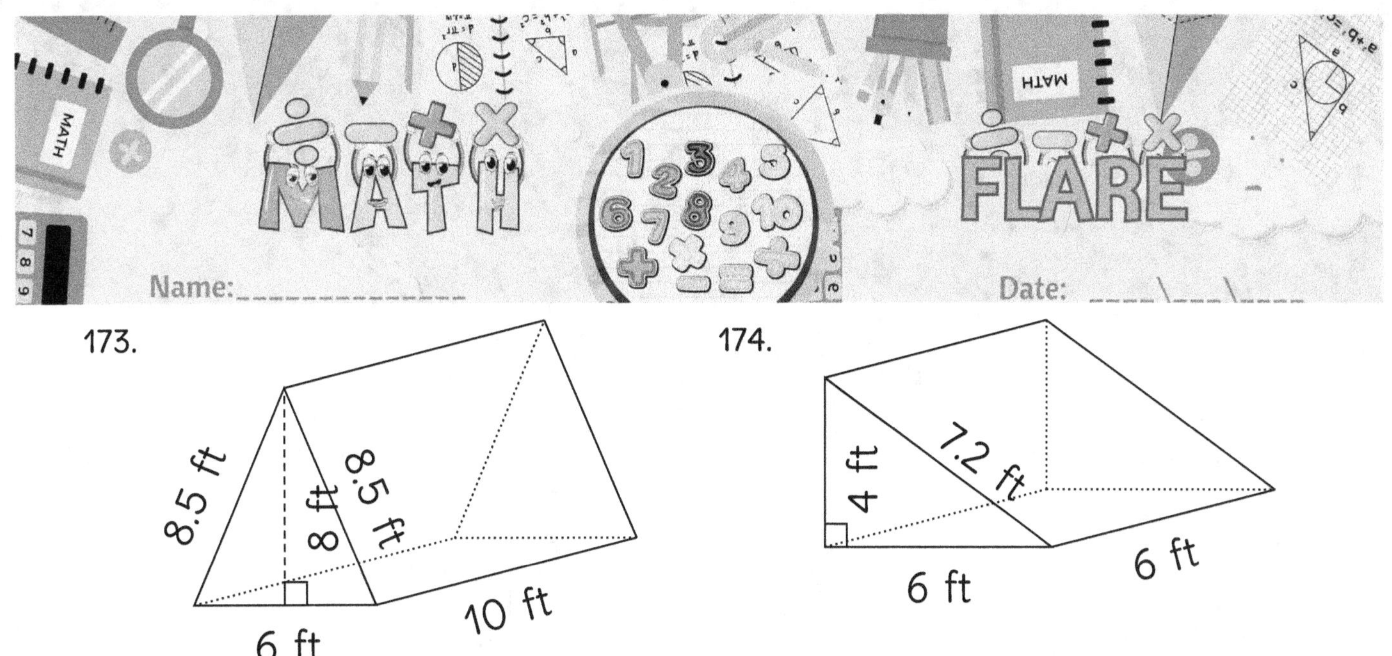

173.

174.

175.

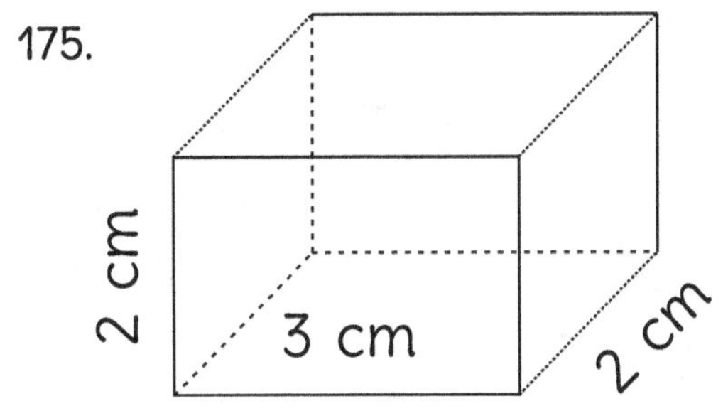

176.

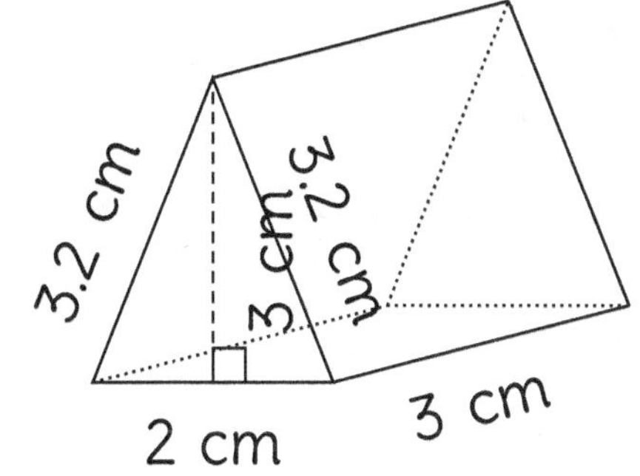

177.

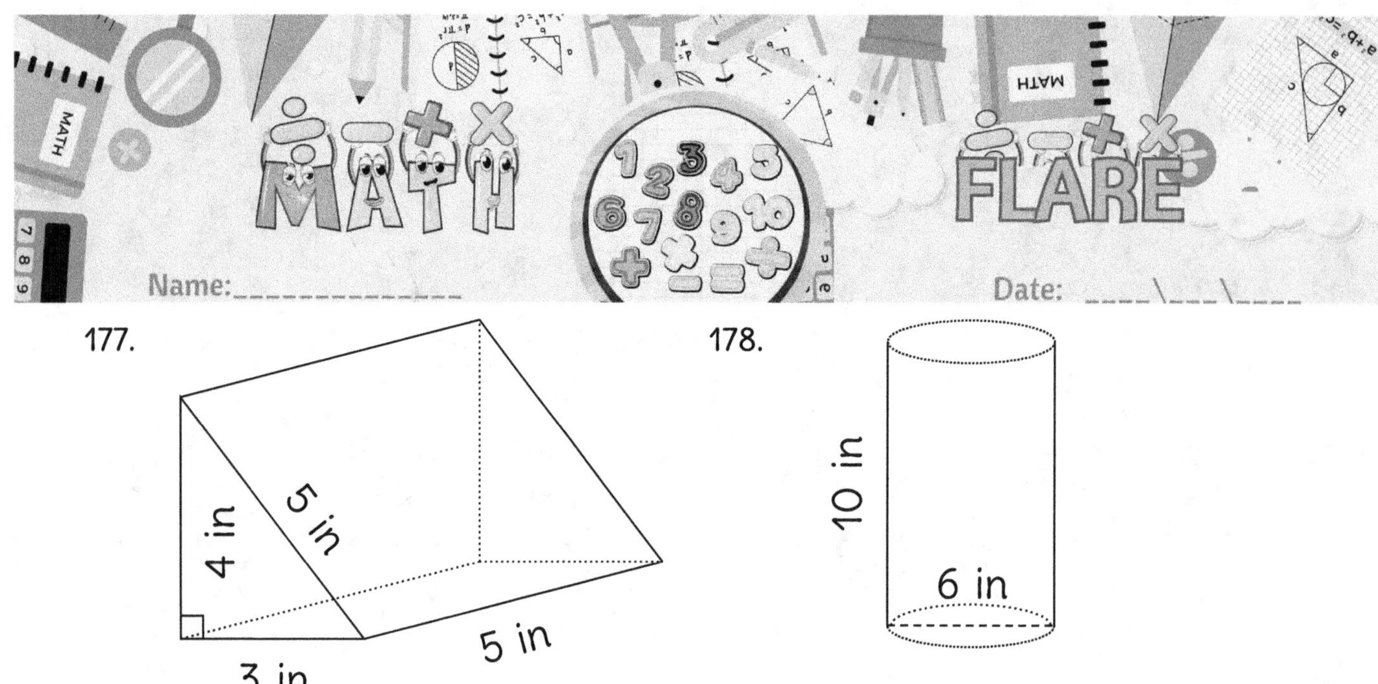

179.

180.

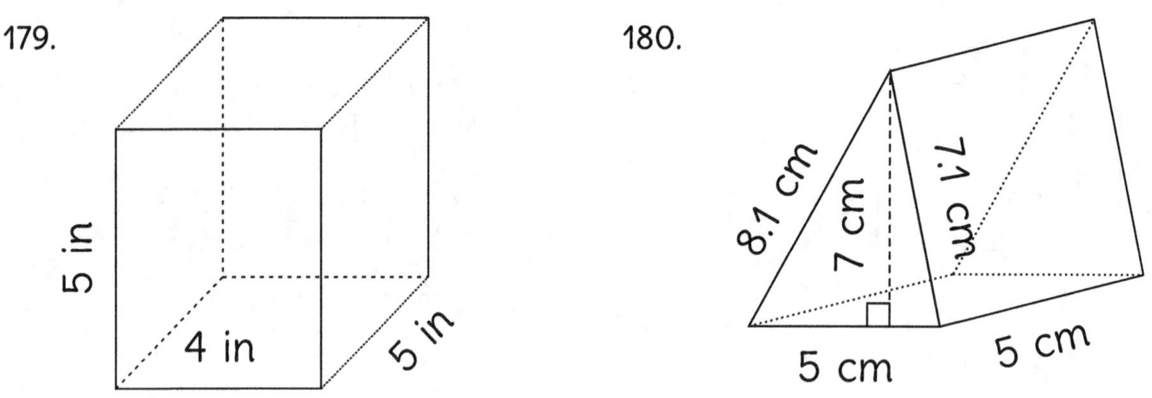

181.

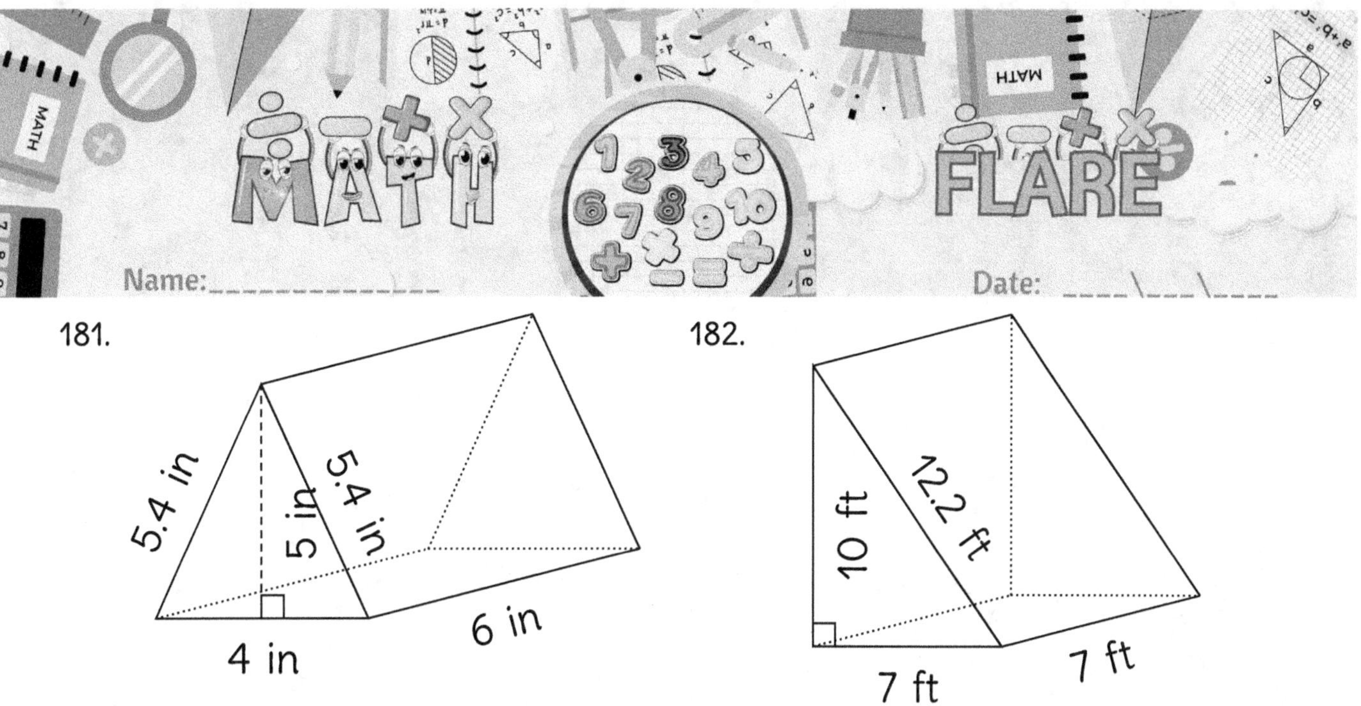

182.

183.

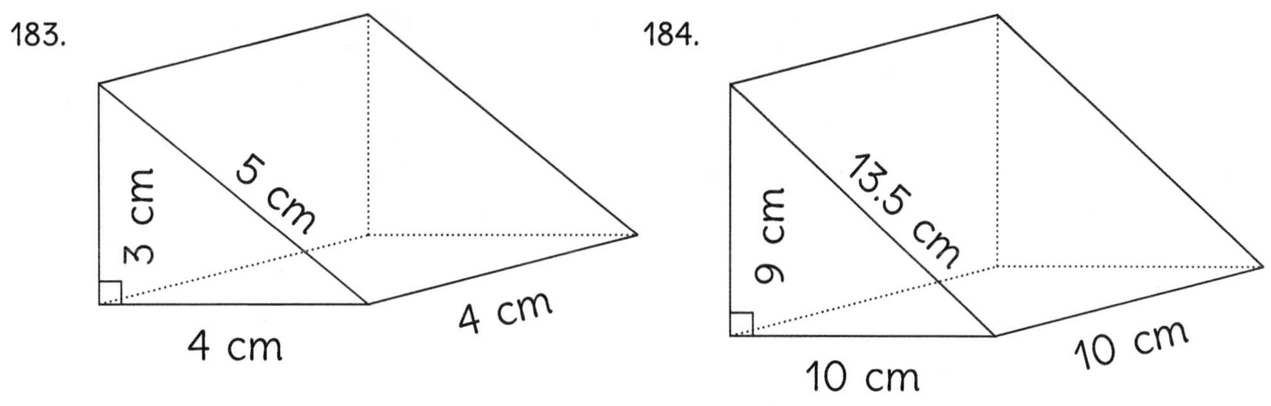

184.

185.

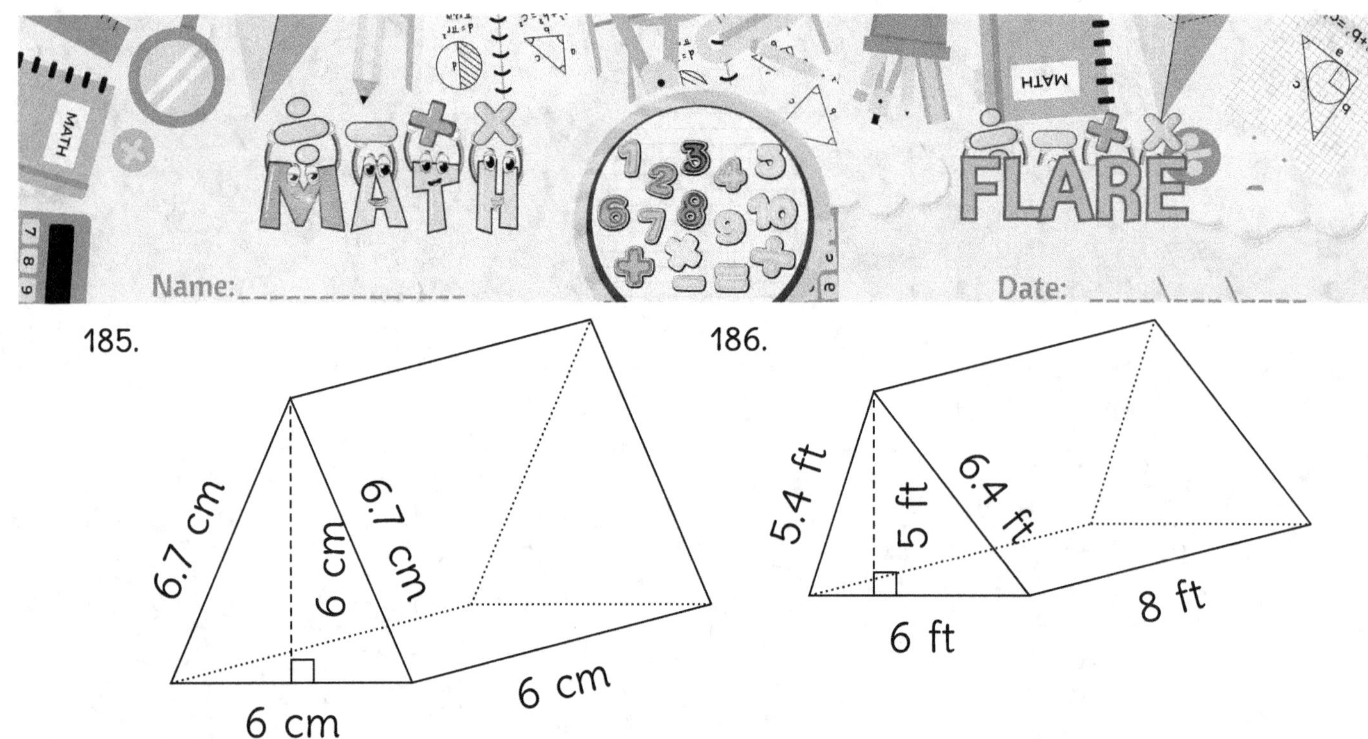

186.

187.

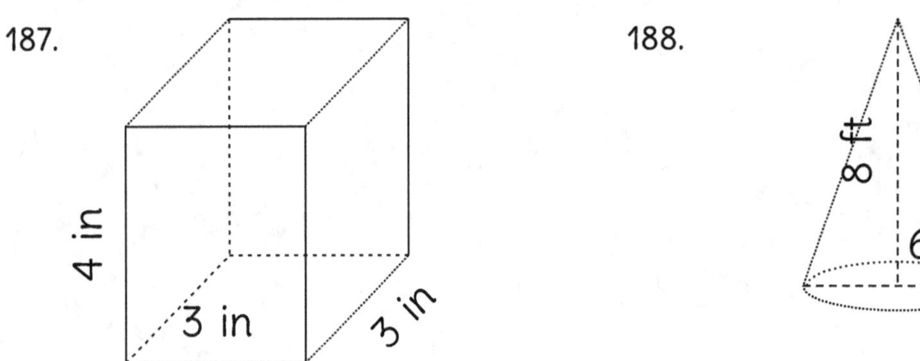

188.

189.
5.8 in
5 in
5.8 in
6 in
5 in
190.
5 in
8 in

191.

5.4 in
5 in
5.4 in
4 in
6 in
192.
2 cm
3 cm
4 cm

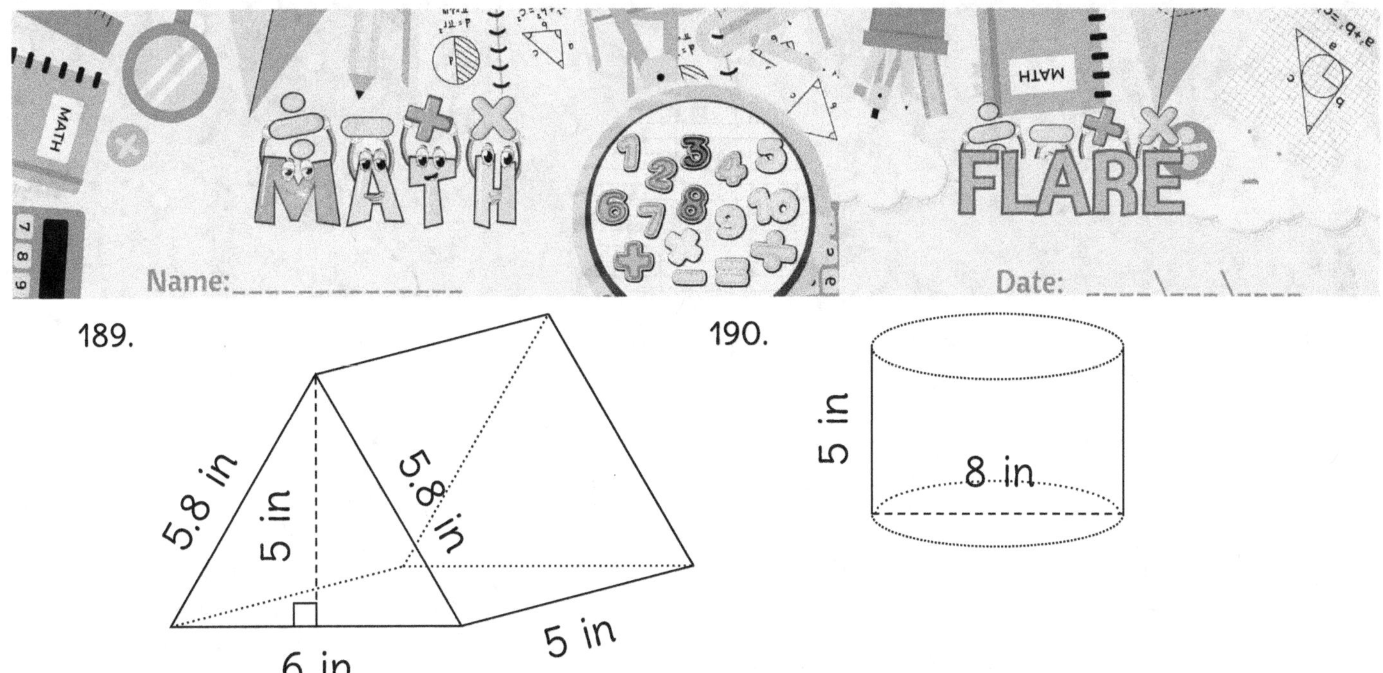

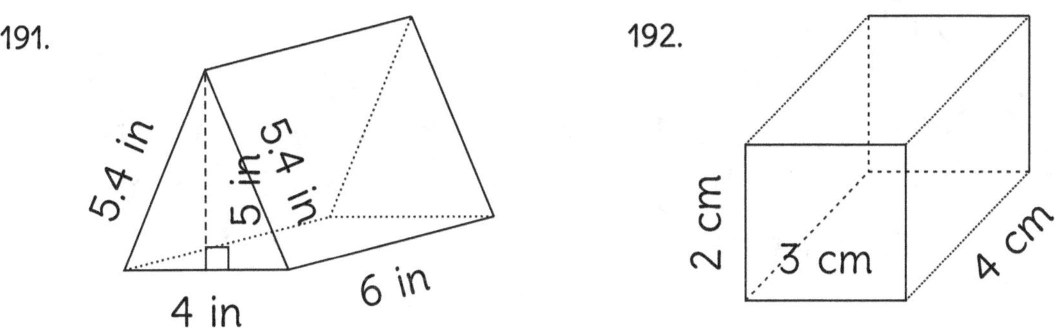

Name:
Date:
193.
6 ft
6 ft
9 ft
194.
8.1 cm
7 cm
8.1 cm
8 cm
8 cm

195.

8.5 ft
6 ft
6 ft
7 ft
196.
6 in
10 in
8 in
6 in

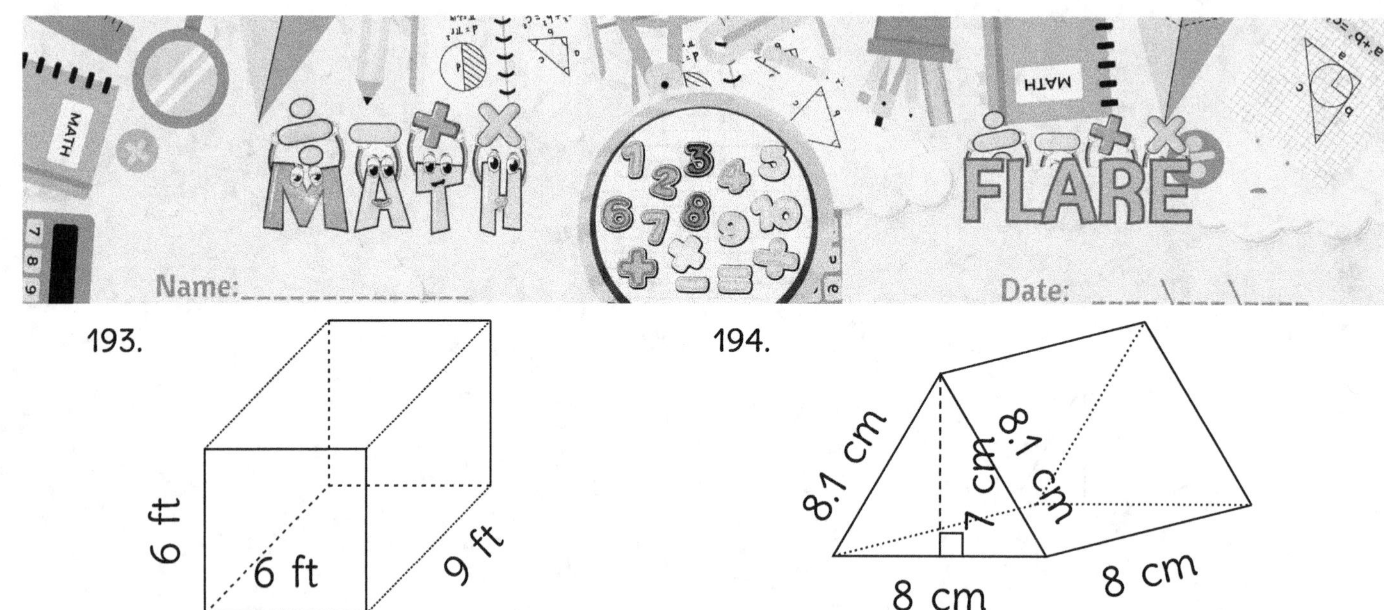

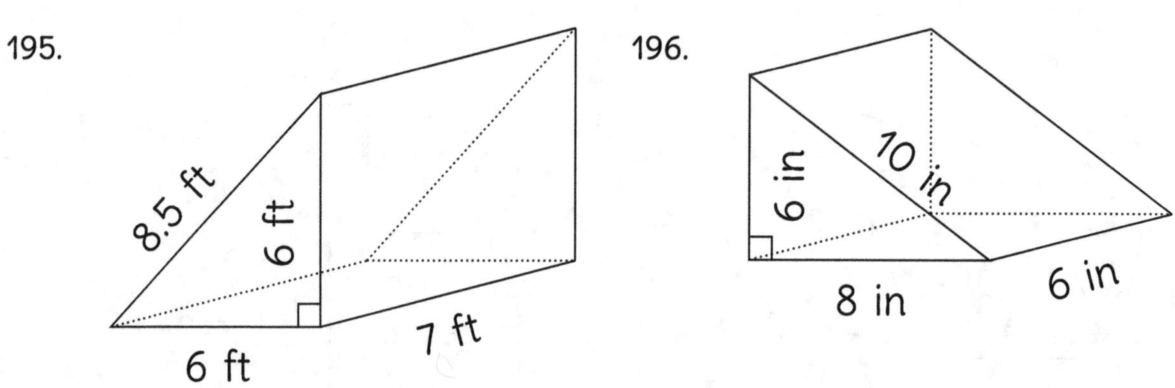

197.

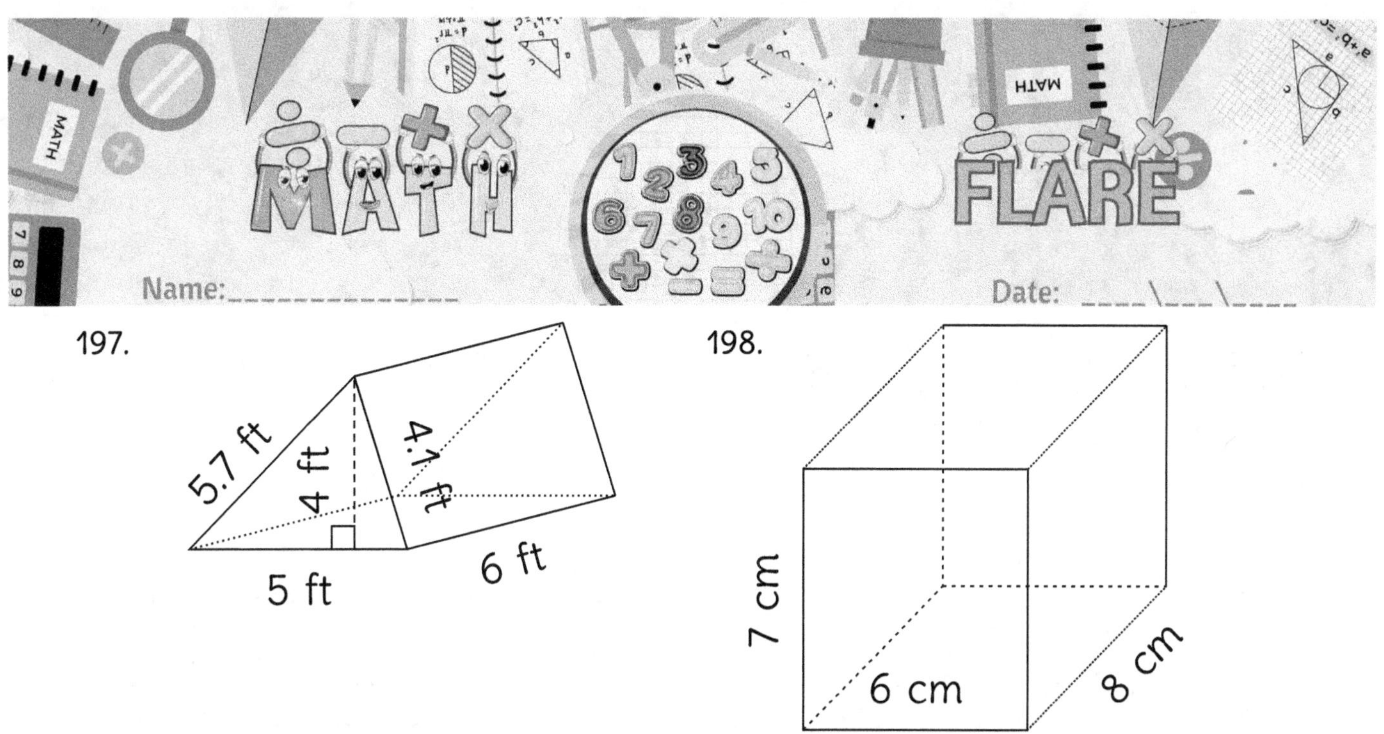

198.

199.

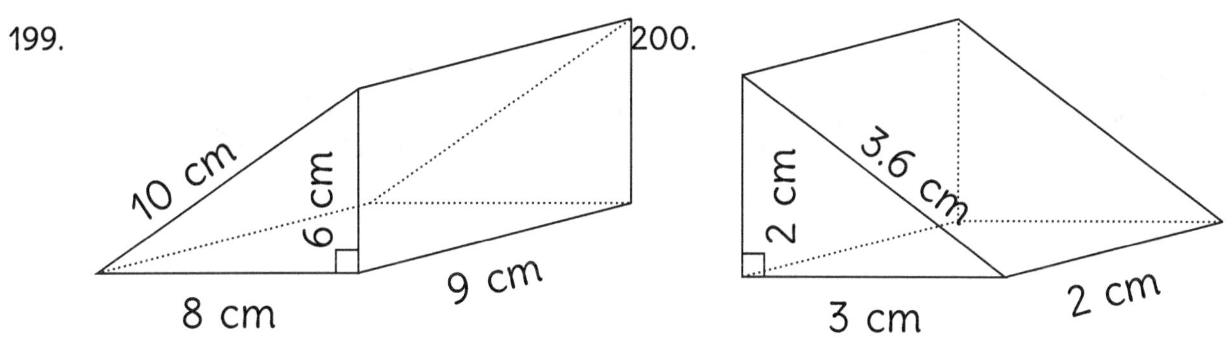

200.

Pythagorean Theorem

Find the length of the side.

201. 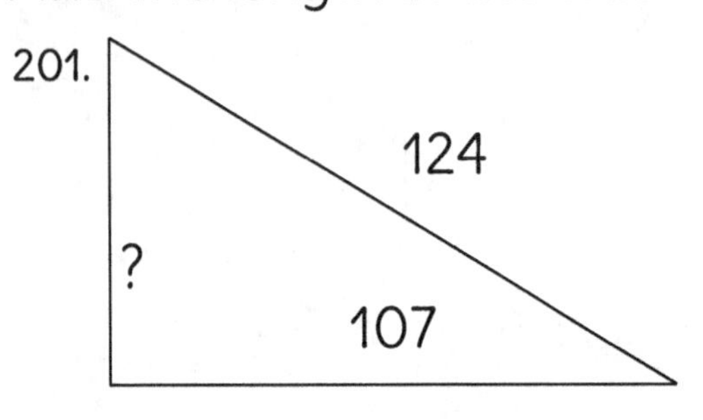

____

202. 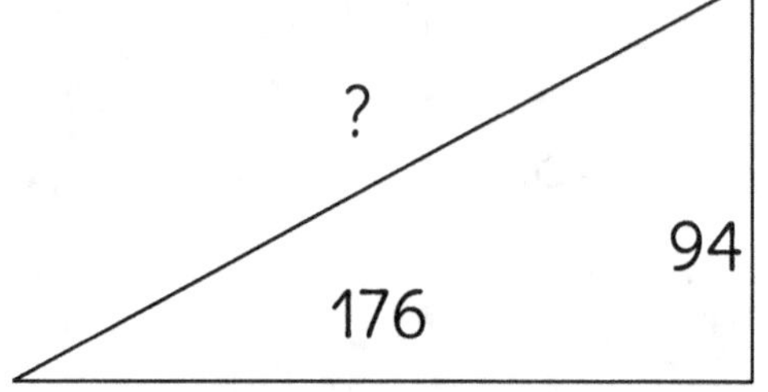

____

203.

____

204. 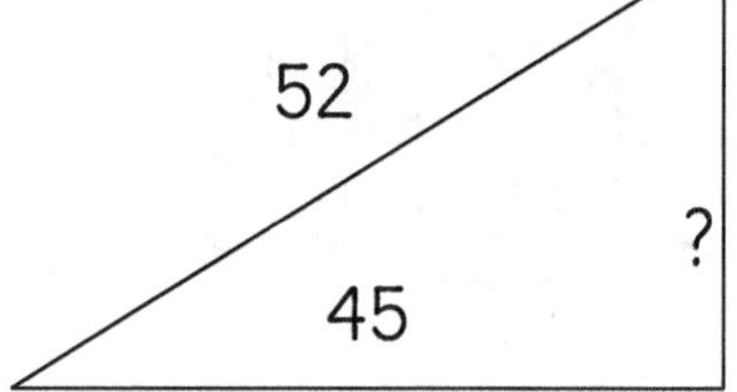

____

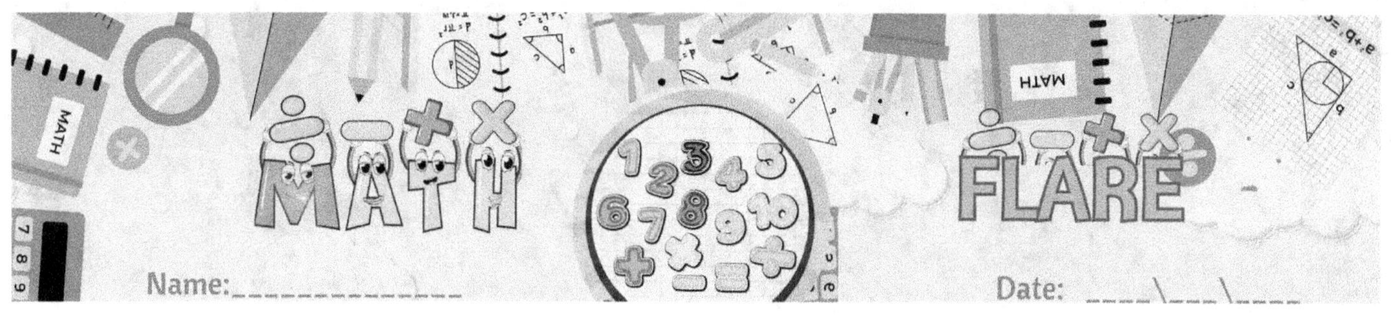

205.

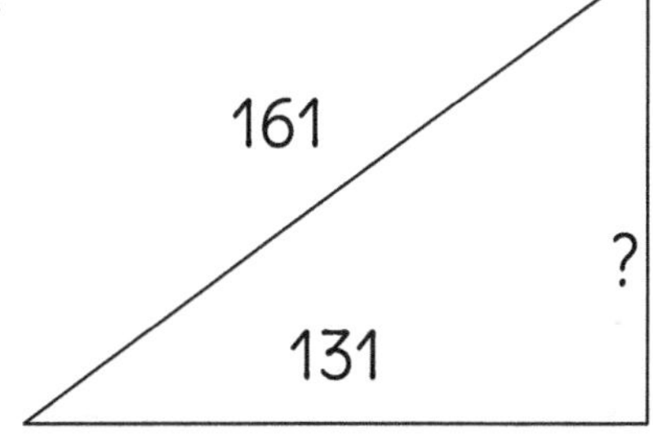

____

206.

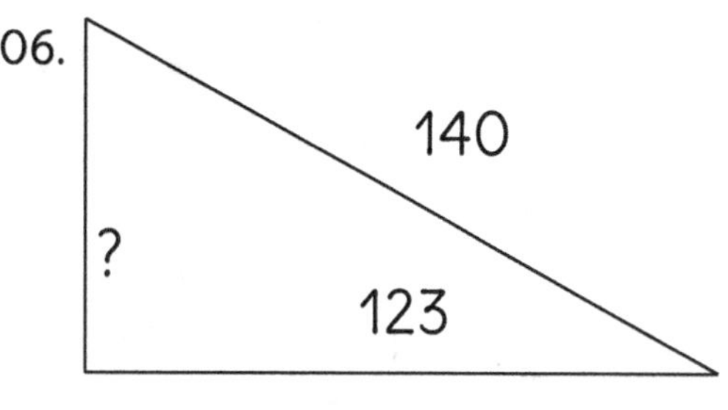

____

207.

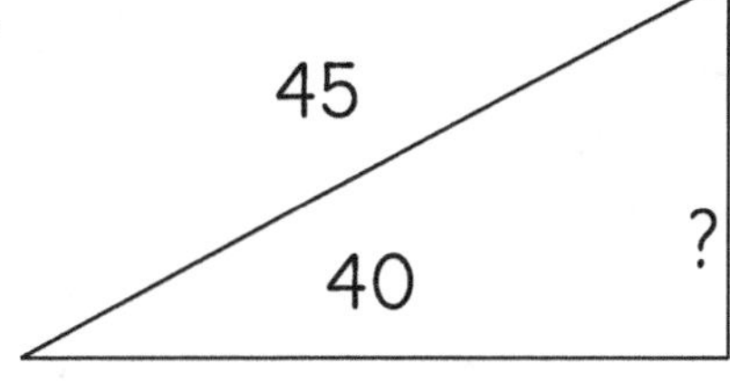

____

208.

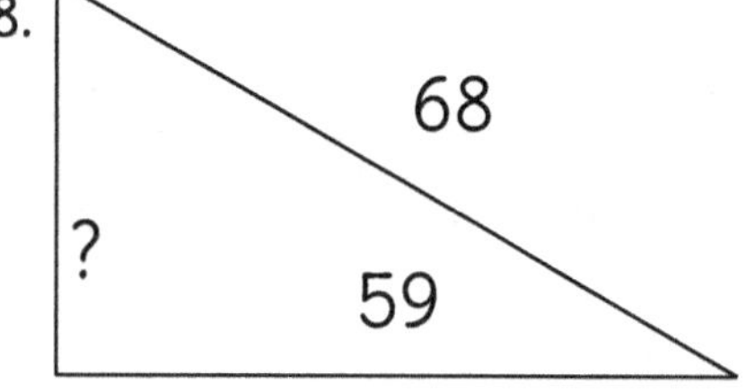

____

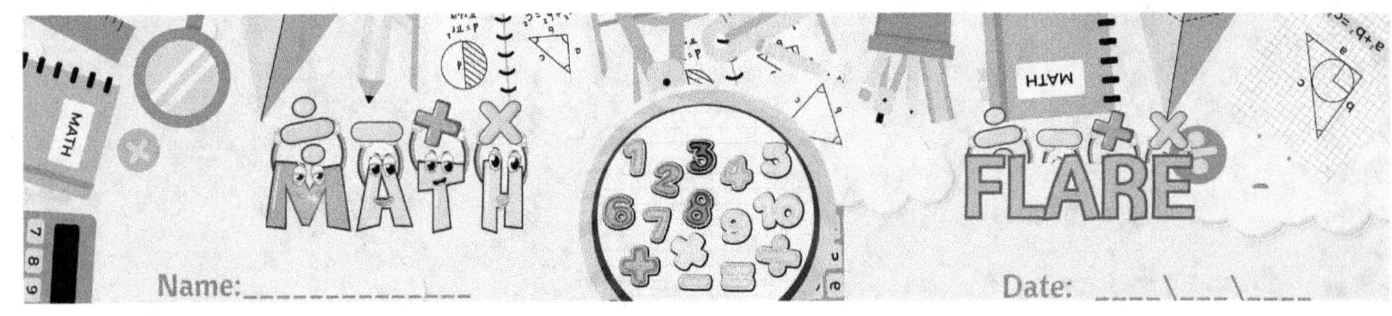

209. 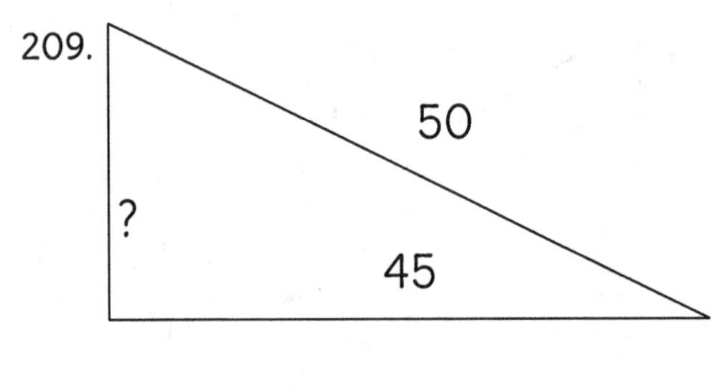

50

?

45

____

210. 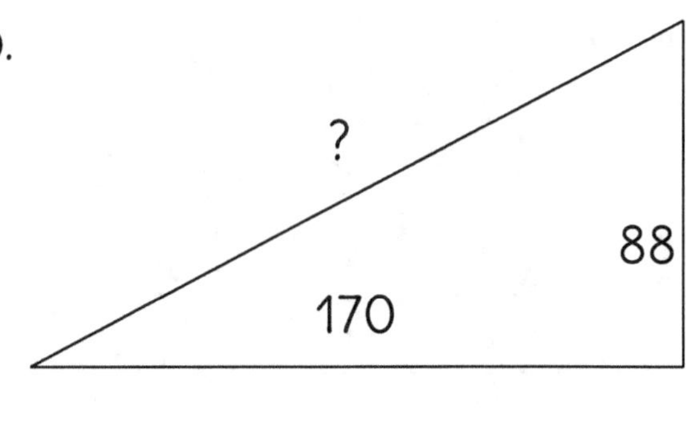

?

88

170

____

211. 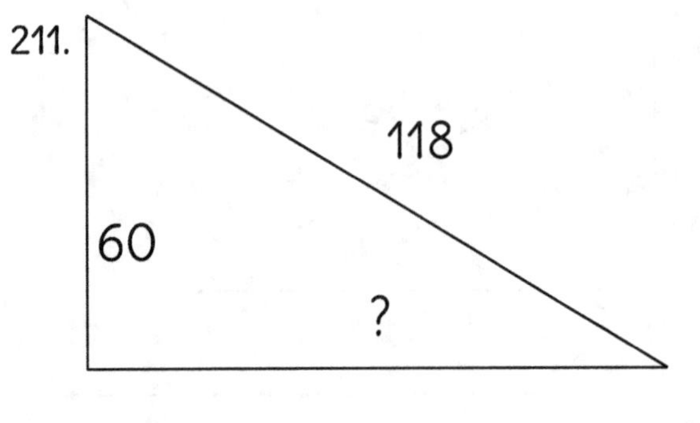

118

60

?

____

212. 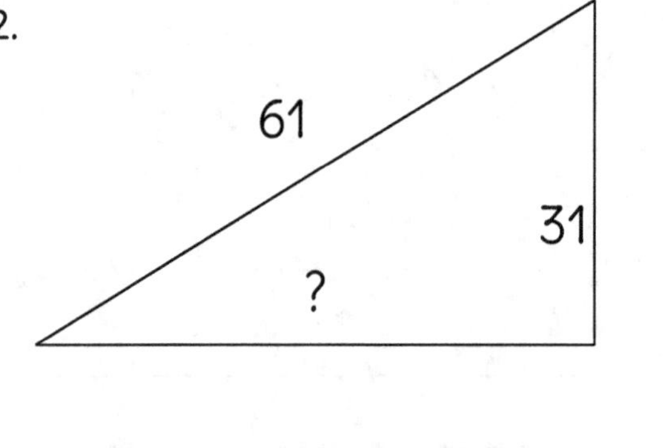

61

31

?

____

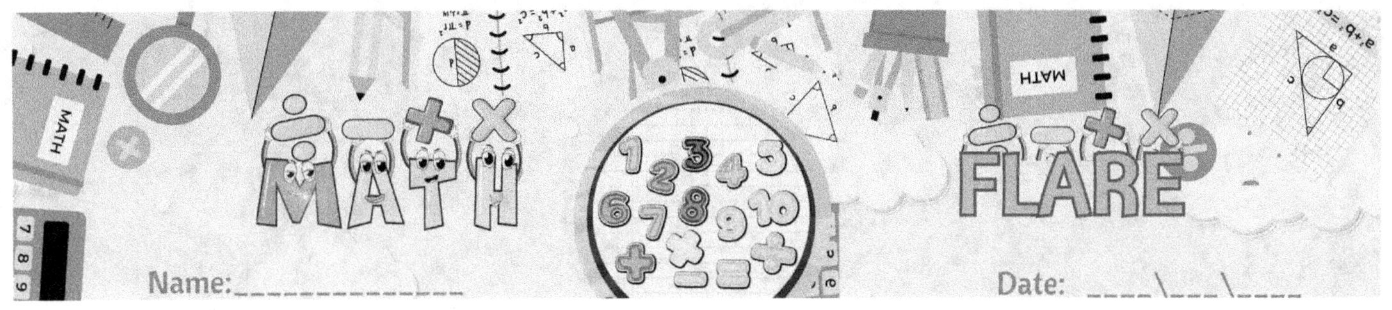

213.

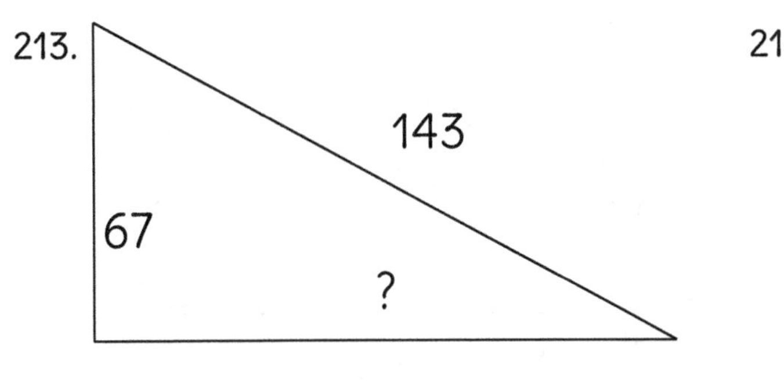

____

214.

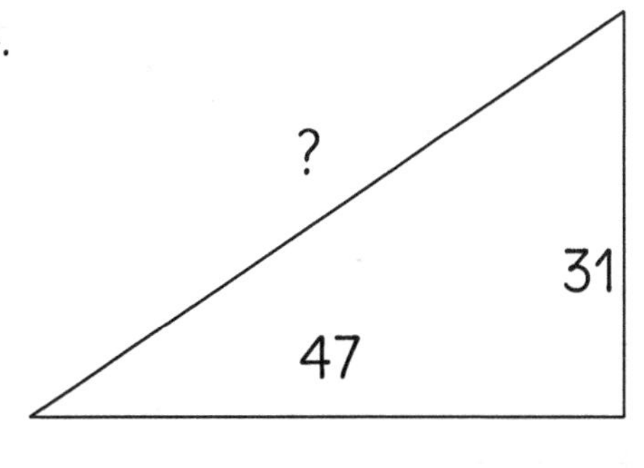

____

215.

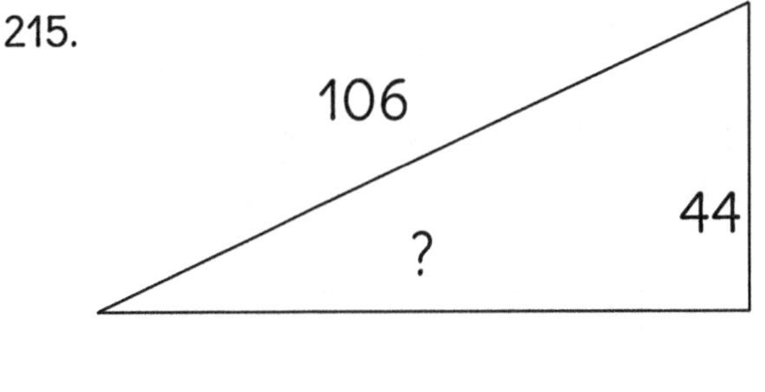

____

216.

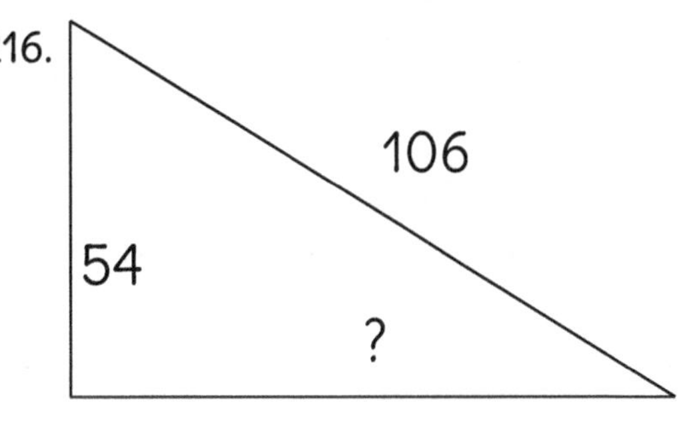

____

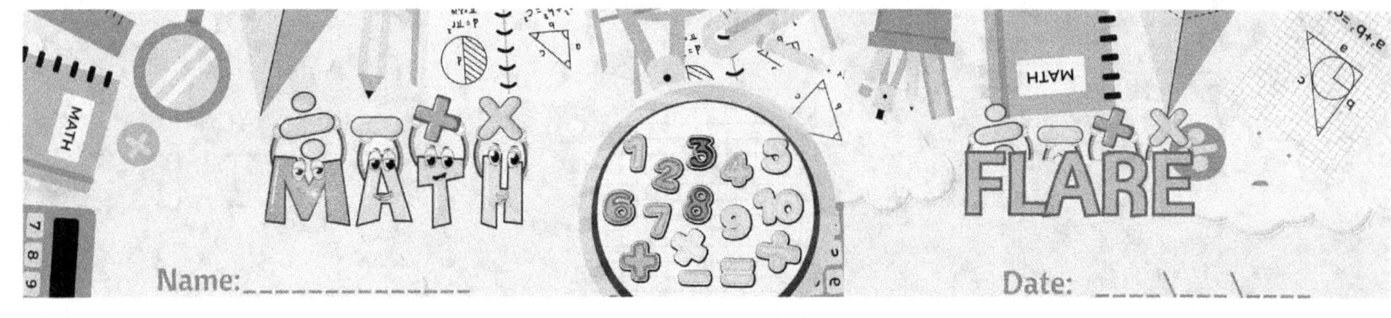

217.

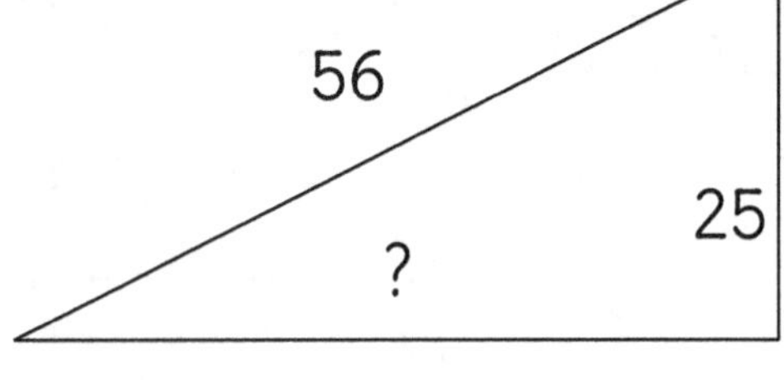

____

218.

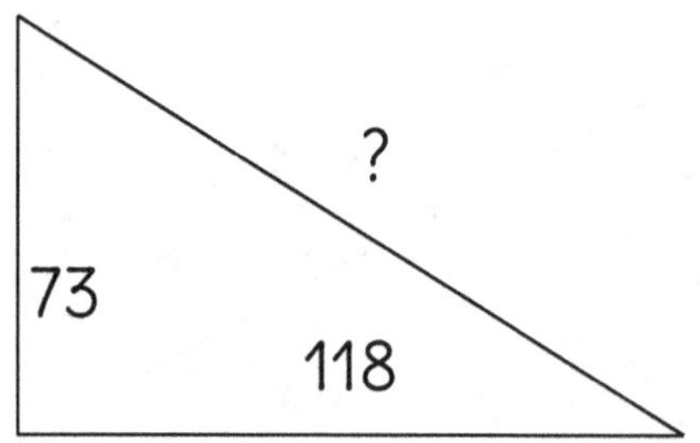

____

219.

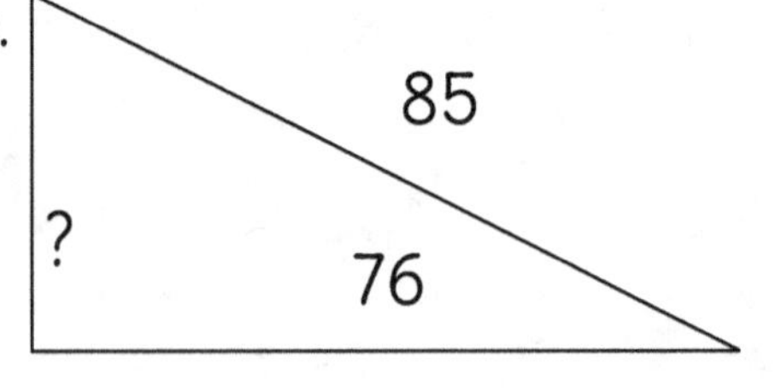

____

220.

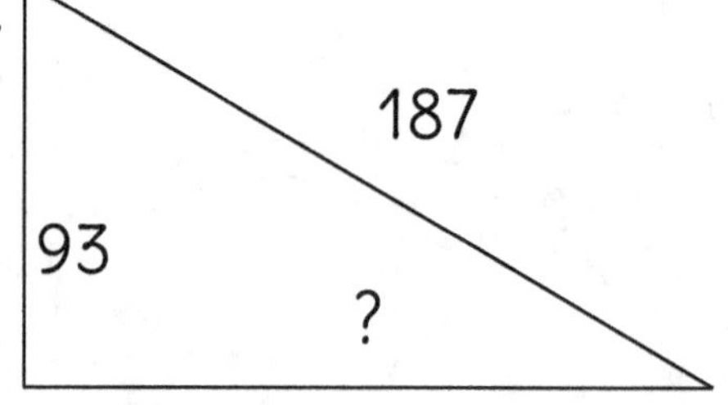

____

ANSWERS

Page 1: Mean, Median, Mode, and Range

1. Mean = 50, Median = 56.5, Mode = none, Range = 78

2. Mean = 51, Median = 48, Mode = none, Range = 91

3. Mean = 56.667, Median = 48.5, Mode = none, Range = 69

4. Mean = 48.714, Median = 42, Mode = none, Range = 83

5. Mean = 53, Median = 49.5, Mode = none, Range = 69

6. Mean = 31.143, Median = 33, Mode = none, Range = 34

7. Mean = 58.333, Median = 70, Mode = none, Range = 68

8. Mean = 41.571, Median = 37, Mode = none, Range = 96

9. Mean = 64, Median = 72, Mode = none, Range = 59

10. Mean = 39.714, Median = 49, Mode = none, Range = 62

11. Mean = 58.333, Median = 70.5, Mode = none, Range = 93

12. Mean = 46.714, Median = 53, Mode = none, Range = 78

13. Mean = 28.143, Median = 20, Mode = none, Range = 93

14. Mean = 71.667, Median = 67, Mode = none, Range = 51

15. Mean = 53, Median = 47.5, Mode = none, Range = 78

16. Mean = 36.833, Median = 34, Mode = none, Range = 68

17. Mean = 50.857, Median = 35, Mode = none, Range = 92

18. Mean = 50.167, Median = 46.5, Mode = none, Range = 60

19. Mean = 35.857, Median = 35, Mode = none, Range = 73

20. Mean = 41, Median = 27, Mode = none, Range = 89

21. Mean = 50.714, Median = 57, Mode = none, Range = 71

22. Mean = 52.667, Median = 51, Mode = none, Range = 84

23. Mean = 52.5, Median = 60.5, Mode = none, Range = 50

24. Mean = 77, Median = 78, Mode = 97, Range = 62

25. Mean = 41.167, Median = 45, Mode = none, Range = 89

26. Mean = 55.714, Median = 58, Mode = none, Range = 79

27. Mean = 60.333, Median = 53.5, Mode = 46, Range = 37

28. Mean = 51.143, Median = 55, Mode = none, Range = 75

29. Mean = 54.833, Median = 52.5, Mode = 34, Range = 46

30. Mean = 65, Median = 75, Mode = none, Range = 88

31. Mean = 48.167, Median = 39, Mode = none, Range = 86

32. Mean = 41.167, Median = 31.5, Mode = none, Range = 76

33. Mean = 63.667, Median = 75, Mode = none, Range = 76

34. Mean = 54.167, Median = 60.5, Mode = none, Range = 88

35. Mean = 60, Median = 73, Mode = none, Range = 85

36. Mean = 46.667, Median = 38, Mode = 26, Range = 74

37. Mean = 51.286, Median = 53, Mode = none, Range = 66

38. Mean = 46.714, Median = 46, Mode = none, Range = 81

39. Mean = 51.571, Median = 45, Mode = none, Range = 80

40. Mean = 63, Median = 69.5, Mode = none, Range = 95

41. Mean = 64.333, Median = 75, Mode = none, Range = 71

42. Mean = 39.286, Median = 43, Mode = none, Range = 82

43. Mean = 37.286, Median = 34, Mode = none, Range = 56

44. Mean = 45, Median = 49.5, Mode = 60, Range = 48

45. Mean = 38.833, Median = 23, Mode = none, Range = 95

46. Mean = 37.286, Median = 40, Mode = none, Range = 62

47. Mean = 64.5, Median = 75.5, Mode = none, Range = 62

48. Mean = 64.333, Median = 74, Mode = 92, Range = 82

49. Mean = 38.333, Median = 34, Mode = none, Range = 45

50. Mean = 27.833, Median = 17.5, Mode = none, Range = 71

51. Mean = 33.429, Median = 27, Mode = none, Range = 84

52. Mean = 50.429, Median = 59, Mode = none, Range = 84

53. Mean = 48.833, Median = 42.5, Mode = none, Range = 78

54. Mean = 57.143, Median = 60, Mode = none, Range = 84

55. Mean = 52.143, Median = 47, Mode = none, Range = 96

56. Mean = 55.429, Median = 58, Mode = 58, Range = 36

57. Mean = 49.857, Median = 46, Mode = 46, Range = 88

58. Mean = 37.667, Median = 39, Mode = 68, Range = 64

59. Mean = 46.833, Median = 35, Mode = 35, Range = 76

60. Mean = 27.833, Median = 18, Mode = 3, Range = 81

Page 16: Area and Perimeter

61. P=22 A=30

62. P=16 A=15

63. P=17 A=13.62

64. P=26 A=42

65. P=32 A=44

66. P=54 A=140

67. P=19 A=22

68. P=48 A=110.85

69. P=26 A=42

70. P=50 A=116

71. P=56 A=152

72. P=42 A=73

73. P=44 A=120

74. P=30 A=56

75. P=33 A=45

76. P=30 A=30

77. P=31 A=45.18

78. P=18 A=15.59

79. P=34 A=54.55

80. P=48 A=97.5

81. P=64 A=192

82. P=38 A=90

83. P=39 A=65

84. P=36 A=81

85. P=60 A=210

86. P=52 A=88

87. P=46 A=103

88. P=51 A=125.14

89. P=34 A=46

90. P=42 A=78

91. P=50 A=144

92. P=15 A=10.82

93. P=40 A=79

94. P=54 A=182

95. P=43 A=104

96. P=20 A=18

97. P=44 A=84.5

98. P=46 A=107

99. P=68 A=288

100. P=29 A=33.12

101. P=62 A=123

102. P=48 A=124

103. P=60 A=225

104. P=52 A=156

105. P=54 A=138

106. P=23 A=20

107. P=26 A=28

108. P=30 A=56

109. P=31 A=40.5

110. P=36 A=62.35

111. P=56 A=168

112. P=50 A=54

113. P=64 A=200

114. P=34 A=48

115. P=27 A=31.5

116. P=50 A=143

117. P=36 A=65

118. P=30 A=43.3

119. P=25 A=28

120. P=61 A=161.5

121. P=27 A=42   122. P=78 A=168   123. P=28 A=40

124. P=58 A=136   125. P=54 A=112   126. P=51 A=112

127. P=34 A=63   128. P=51 A=112   129. P=28 A=49

130. P=38 A=80   131. P=38 A=73   132. P=48 A=68

133. P=36 A=62.35   134. P=19 A=22   135. P=31 A=34.32

136. P=52 A=140   137. P=48 A=144   138. P=42 A=84.87

139. P=30 A=40   140. P=40 A=82

Page 36: Volume and Surface Area

141. $V=230.91$ in³ in³ SA=209 in² in²

142. $V=34$ in³ in³ SA=50 in² in²

143. $V=240$ ft³ ft³ SA=236 ft² ft²

144. $V=628.32$ ft³ ft³ SA=408 ft² ft²

145. $V=170$ cm³ cm³ SA=193 cm² cm²

146. $V=12$ cm³ cm³ SA=32 cm² cm²

147. $V=7$ cm³ cm³ SA=23 cm² cm²

148. $V=39$ cm³ cm³ SA=71 cm² cm²

149. $V=113$ in³ in³ SA=113 in² in²

150. $V=120$ cm³ cm³ SA=148 cm² cm²

151. $V=105$ ft³ ft³ SA=152.0 ft² ft²

152. $V=24$ ft³ ft³ SA=55.0 ft² ft²

153. $V=288$ ft³ ft³ SA=264 ft² ft²

154. V=18 ft³ ft³ SA=42 ft² ft²

155. V=445.32 ft³ ft³ SA=325 ft² ft²

156. V=75.40 cm³ cm³ SA=101 cm² cm²

157. V=192 cm³ cm³ SA=230.4 cm² cm²

158. V=50 ft³ ft³ SA=94.0 ft² ft²

159. V=120 in³ in³ SA=148 in² in²

160. V=770 cm³ cm³ SA=514 cm² cm²

161. V=66 cm³ cm³ SA=100 cm² cm²

162. V=9 ft³ ft³ SA=31.8 ft² ft²

163. V=196 in³ in³ SA=210 in² in²

164. V=36 in³ in³ SA=66 in² in²

165. V=33 in³ in³ SA=64 in² in²

166. V=196 ft³ ft³ SA=232.2 ft² ft²

167. V=141.37 cm³ cm³ SA=151 cm² cm²

168. V=855.30 cm³ cm³ SA=501 cm² cm²

169. V=13 ft³ ft³ SA=35 ft² ft²

170. V=103 ft³ ft³ SA=134 ft² ft²

171. V=448 ft³ ft³ SA=352 ft² ft²

172. V=168 cm³ cm³ SA=186 cm² cm²

173. V=240 ft³ ft³ SA=278.0 ft² ft²

174. V=72 ft³ ft³ SA=127.2 ft² ft²

175. V=12 cm³ cm³ SA=32 cm² cm²

176. V=9 cm³ cm³ SA=31.2 cm² cm²

177. V=30 in³ in³ SA=72 in² in²

178. V=282.74 in³ in³ SA=245 in² in²

179. V=100 in³ in³ SA=130 in² in²

180. V=88 cm³ cm³ SA=136.0 cm² cm²

181. V=60 in³ in³ SA=108.8 in² in²

182. V=245 ft³ ft³ SA=274.4 ft² ft²

183. V=24 cm³ cm³ SA=60 cm² cm²

184. V=450 cm³ cm³ SA=415.0 cm² cm²

185. V=108 cm³ cm³ SA=152.4 cm² cm²

186. V=120 ft³ ft³ SA=172.4 ft² ft²

187. V=36 in³ in³ SA=66 in² in²

188. V=75 ft³ ft³ SA=109 ft² ft²

189. V=75 in³ in³ SA=118.0 in² in²

190. V=251.33 in³ in³ SA=226 in² in²

191. V=60 in³ in³ SA=108.8 in² in²

192. V=24 cm³ cm³ SA=52 cm² cm²

193. V=324 ft³ ft³ SA=288 ft² ft²

194. V=224 cm³ cm³ SA=249.6 cm² cm²

195. V=126 ft³ ft³ SA=179.5 ft² ft²

196. V=144 in³ in³ SA=192 in² in²

197. V=60 ft³ ft³ SA=108.8 ft² ft²

198. V=336 cm³ cm³ SA=292 cm² cm²

199. V=216 cm³ cm³ SA=264 cm² cm²

200. V=6 cm³ cm³ SA=23.2 cm² cm²

Page 51: Pythagorean Theorem

201. S=62.666	202. S=199.529	203. S=160.879	204. S=26.058
205. S=93.595	206. S=66.866	207. S=20.616	208. S=33.808
209. S=21.794	210. S=191.426	211. S=101.607	212. S=52.536
213. S=126.333	214. S=56.303	215. S=96.437	216. S=91.214
217. S=50.110	218. S=138.755	219. S=38.066	220. S=162.234